THE NAKED
BUDDHA

A simple explanation of a 'new' old religion

Venerable Adrienne Howley

HEALTH HARMONY

THE NAKED BUDDHA

First Indian Edition: 2003

Reprinted by Special Arangement with Transworld Publishers, A division of Random House Australia Pty Ltd., 20 Alfred Street, Milsons Point, NSW 2061, http://www.randomhouse.com.au.

Howley, Adrienne.
The naked Buddha : a simple explanation of a 'new' old religion.
Sale within Indian Subcontinent

Price: **Rs. 120.00**

Published by Kuldeep Jain for

HEALTH  **HARMONY**
an imprint of

B. Jain Publishers (P) Ltd.
1921, Street No. 10, Chuna Mandi,
Paharganj, New Delhi 110 055 (INDIA)
Phones: 2358 0800, 2358 1100, 2358 1300, 2358 3100
Fax: 011-2358 0471; *Email:* bjain@vsnl.com
Website: www.healthharmonybooks.com

Printed in India by
Gopsons Papers Ltd.
A-14 Sector 60
Noida 201 301

ISBN : 81-8056-343-X   BOOK CODE : BH-5712

CONTENTS

O Bhikkhus, I say that volition (intentional action)
is Karma.

Anguttara Nikaya VI

PREFACE

Each of us has made, for personal use, several hats, wearing them on different occasions, for different audiences and according to our immediate disposition. When I began to write this book, I might have worn my nursing hat, or my nautical hat, or my elderly lady–community worker hat. None of these would have put me in the right mood to create the work I now wish to offer my readers.

The 'hat' I am wearing as I write is, in fact, the hatless, shaven head of a fully ordained bhikkhuni (usually referred to as a Buddhist nun) or, as the Japanese have it, ama hoshi (nun–priest).

The reason for the following pages is the grave misunderstanding of Buddhism prevailing in the West and the need for clarification in view of the introduction into our society of Buddhist communities from various countries. In Australia, we have now a great influx of not only a different type of religion but one practised by a different racial group. We are in the position of either trying to understand a religion as well as a culture, each alien to us, or of unfortunately, out of fear and lack of understanding, becoming intolerant—sometimes in the extreme.

The title of this book illustrates my attempt to strip away stereotypical views of Buddhism, laying reverently and respectfully to one side the cultural trappings under which the original idea becomes almost hidden from view. In many temples one sees the basic Buddha statues swathed in rich brocades and festooned with jewels—mock and real—by devotees. Some statues are firstly

covered in gold leaf or at least gold paint. The hair and
facial features are highlighted. All is done with loving
care, often in the hope of gaining 'merit', yet the outsider
may see a form of idol worship rather than reverence for
the Teacher. Offerings are like silent prayers of praise and
gratitude for what the Buddha taught.

All religions have devotional adherents among their
followers; it is a matter of individual psychological make-
up. We seek, and hope to find, what we most need. The
devotee needs to show devotion, hence the offerings to
the statue, which represents the focus of the devotee's
aspirations. As I am not the devotional type, I seek to
strip the Buddha of added layers and covering and get
down, as closely as I can, to what he really thought and
taught. My way is not better than that of the devotee, only
different.

My aim in this book is to inspire religious, racial and
cultural tolerance through understanding. I hope to
achieve this through explanations of religious and philosophical points of view based on my own studies and
experiences. My reason for attempting this is to help head
off, in this country, the type of 'religious' strife and persecution seen in so many parts of our world today—and
also, of course, because the subject of Buddhism is an
interesting and topical one.

What I find most interesting about Buddhism is that
the Buddha taught for forty years and then invited his
followers not to believe a word he had told them until
they had investigated it for themselves. Here was no guru
demanding instant, unquestioned obedience and devotion, unlike many who set themselves up as teachers of
Buddhism today. He did not teach daydreams and peace
of mind. He did not teach the search for the *Self* or how

to avoid an unfortunate reincarnation. He taught mental alertness, constant investigation (shades of Julius Sumner Miller—'Why is it so?') and clear-sightedness, amongst other matters.

Although I am a nun, I do not profess to be religious and may disappoint those seeking mystery and magic and messages from 'beyond'. Buddha did not deal in such ideas. I have based my own thinking on the earliest material about him that I have been able to discover, the original excavations having been done for me by scholars more qualified and more easily able to do so.

I sign this preface wearing three of my hats which are, nevertheless, the same one.

Adrienne Howley
Venerable Tenzin Galdan
Venerable Thich Nu Tri Anh

Lorn, NSW Australia
March 1998

ACKNOWLEDGMENTS

I cannot thank, by name, the many scholars and philosophers whose works have contributed to my present level of knowledge of my subject, nor all the kind teachers who have spoken with me face to face. What is written here is perhaps best described as a distillation of my understanding of what they sought to teach, now strained through both my own experience and—where mistakes occur—my own lack of comprehension.

My sincere thanks go to those lay and Sangha members who remained my friends despite my often seemingly unorthodox views and my tendency to find something amusing in what, to many, may be unquestionable sacred truths.

I wish to thank my sons for accepting me as I am and for the title of this book. When it was first suggested to me I laughed, but very soon I realised that The Naked Buddha was exactly what I was trying to describe.

A thousand thanks to my cousin Norma and her daughter Andrea, without whose computer expertise neither my manuscript nor my partial typescript would have been legible. And to Deb, who even gave me an Apple Macintosh computer in the hope that I might learn to use it and do the job for myself—I didn't. A special thank you to my editors at Transworld, who made so much sense with their wise suggestions.

1

THE HISTORICAL BUDDHA

Who was he? When and where did he live and
die? How and why did he become a teacher
and what did he teach?

W ho was this person whom so many people refer to
as the Buddha, Lord Buddha or Buddha Sakyamuni?
What did he do or say that had such a momentous effect on
his own people while he lived and was heard in most parts
of the known world of the time? When and where did this
person live? Where did he travel? Where did his followers
take his teachings? Why did he find it necesary to teach
something new in a land that already had a strong, functioning religious structure in place: Brahminism. Why did
his teachings take so firm a hold at a time when so many
were philosophising deeply about life?

Historical records, modern knowledge of ancient
customs and even archaeology can tell us enough to construct a simple, straightforward picture of the life of the
Buddha. Stories from folklore and stories inspired by
devotion have added a great deal of improbable deco-
ration to the picture—a price paid by anyone who comes
to public notice.

The given name of the Buddha was Siddhartha and his
family name was Gautama. He was the heir to his father
Suddhodana, elected king of the Sakyas, a wealthy clan
whose state lay partly in what is now western Nepal.
Siddhartha was born in about 543 BC, traditionally at the
time of full moon in our month of May. His mother,
Queen Maya, died seven days after his birth, and Maya's
sister, who had been Suddhodana's second wife and was
probably already the mother of Siddhartha's always-
jealous cousin (or half-brother), Davida, became the
baby's foster mother.

Although the child Siddhartha was showered with all
the pleasures his father and the Sakyas could bestow on
him, he grew up to be rather serious-minded. He was
given the best available secular and religious education,
as well as being groomed as the future political and
military leader of his clan.

In India in the sixth century BC, the people were
divided into castes based on skin colour, due to
repeated invasions of light-skinned, blue-eyed people
from the north-west. The invaders forced the indige-
nous population further and further southward and
they, in turn, displaced the earlier inhabitants. Breeding
between invaders and those conquered was responsible
for different skin tones and this, as elsewhere in the
world, tended to categorise people socially. Later, caste

became a matter of birth and, in order of status, was as follows:

Brahmins: hereditary priests of the main Indian religion having Brahma as creator. They were the only possible mediators between the myriad of gods and goddesses, and human beings. None but Brahmins might make sacrifices and read the resulting omens. No-one could rise to be a Brahmin, one had to be born to that status. Brahmins were Brahmins—good, bad or indifferent. They considered themselves of primary importance and grew rich on the offerings from the people, who paid for the priests to perform all the necessary ceremonies to placate the gods, and all the rituals for betrothals, marriages and deaths, and to read the future from the stars.

Ksatriya: the military and ruling class, whose duties were to guard the people and the land. Many considered the Ksatriya even more important than the Brahmins. In this group were the leaders, chieftains and kings of various areas—rajahs and maharajahs, military captains and political administrators.

Vaisya: merchants and skilled workers. This group comprised traders, businesspeople, and those whose caravans carried all the local news and gossip within their own country and into the countries of their trading partners. They were agriculturalists, tradespeople, workers in metal, stone and fabrics, artists and so on.

Sudra: mostly unskilled workers. These were small, dark-skinned people, probably the original inhabitants of India. They were taken over by Aryan and other invaders over the centuries. Later they came to be called the

Untouchables and were given the most unpleasant tasks to perform, but this was not yet the case in the sixth century BC.

Slaves: usually foreigners and prisoners-of-war. Their circumstances depended on their owners. They might be treated as anything from a friend to a chattel.

One caste did not marry into another, except on rare occasions, as much due to preference as to custom. Brahmins married only Brahmins, considering all others to be of lower caste.

Although the priests held enormous influence over the minds of the people, there were always some people who wished to delve more deeply into the whys and hows of life than what was explained by the existing religion, the tenets of which they regarded as degraded beliefs and superstitions. These persons became the wandering ascetics, who lived in the forests for long periods, fed by devoted followers or living on herbs and fruits. Only during the monsoon period did they need shelter other than the shade of a tree.

Family life in India being of such importance, it became acceptable for men or women to become forest dwellers or wandering seekers-after-wisdom only after family duties had been attended to. Heirs had to be produced, wives and parents provided for if necessary, and the consent of families sought and received. Naturally, many simply absconded from their responsibilities.

As is still the custom in India today, marriage took place quite early in life. At sixteen or even earlier, a boy was—for all physical intents and purposes—considered ready for marriage. Siddhartha Gautama, a Ksatriya, was no exception. At sixteen he was married to his cousin, daughter of the neighbouring clan leader. Her name was Yasodarah, and she brought a rich dowry, part of which consisted of many handmaidens—as was customary for a woman of her class.

Siddhartha led the life of any healthy young man of wealth in a loving, indulgent family. It is possible daughters were born to Yasodarah and even sons to his concubines, but daughters, unless they personally achieved fame, were rarely listed in the history of that time. The first son of the first wife became the heir. Most stories agree that Siddhartha was nearly twenty-nine when Yasodarah bore a son, although possibly this may have happened at an earlier date. The story of renunciation in leaving a *baby* son may be more folktale than history. The Sakya prince's duty was done. The child was named Rahula and later he would become one of his father's disciples and a monk or Sangha member.

Traditional stories state that during the Buddha's childhood he was sheltered from the unpleasant facts of old age, sickness and death. This was his father's scheme for keeping his son safe from the first part of a prophecy given at his birth. The prophecy said that the child would become a great spiritual teacher or a great warrior and leader. Naturally the father hoped his first-born would follow in his own footsteps. Everything that Siddhartha could desire was at hand. He was educated and trained for war and leadership. Eventually, when on a state visit outside the royal precincts, the vigilance of his attendants fell short of the King's instructions and Siddhartha saw all his father had tried to hide from him. When it was explained to him that this was the common lot of humanity, the seed was born in his mind to try to discover the cause of suffering and, if possible, how to overcome it. By the time he was twenty-nine he had made up his mind to begin his search.

For the next six years, as a wandering seeker, Siddhartha Gautama sought the teachings and practices of the leading samanaras (philosophers or holy men) of the day. Some taught indulgence in order to learn disgust for the desires of the body from excessive eating, drinking and sexual practices; some ate only one herb or fruit; some practised self- or other-inflicted torture; some practised all types of yogic exercises and deep trance; and some participated in deep philosophical discussions. From none of these practices did Siddhartha find the answers he sought.

The final practice he underwent at this period was long and drastic fasting. This caused him to become so emaciated and weak that, on entering a stream one morning to bathe, he came close to drowning. He accepted some prepared food, for which his fellow wanderers—five ascetics—scorned him. Then he reviewed his experiences of the past years and realised that none of them had led to the wisdom he sought.

When his health recovered, he made a vow to sit beneath the pipal tree (a type of ficus) and meditate until he either found the wisdom he sought or died. The tree, later to be known as the Bodhi tree, was at Bodh Gaya in India. A slip was taken from the original tree and, since then, before each Bodhi tree dies, a slip is planted on the same spot (slips are exported to other Buddhist countries as well). The place has become, next to Kusinara (where the Buddha died), the most revered place for Buddhist pilgrims.

Siddhartha sat on a heap of grass, in what we call the

lotus position, his palms up on his lap, right on left, and began his momentous quest. For several days he made little headway, wrestling with the temptation to give up. As he was fasting, he even suffered hallucinations. Then, early one morning, when he had no strength to continue, what he sought suddenly became clear to him. It was not a 'miracle', but the result of his own efforts. He had become the Buddha, which means the Enlightened One.

It may be appropriate here to draw attention to the great differences between the Buddha and the leaders of other religions: he was not and never professed to be the off-spring of any god; he did not receive messages and instructions from mysterious sources, angels or demons; he never claimed his was the only way, but only invited those who wished to do so to come and try it. Buddhism is not a proselytising religion. The Dharma—the Buddha's teach-ings, called the law—is taught to individuals or groups who ask for it. The teacher does not seek the student.

The Buddha was not sure if his 'message' would be acceptable to, or understood by, the majority of people, but after consideration he realised that what he had learned could be of immense help to many sentient (con-scious) beings. He decided to share what he had learned, out of compassion for suffering caused by ignorance. His first sermon was to the five ascetics who had mocked him for breaking his long fast. He explained to them his enlightenment, his coming to understand suffering: the cause of suffering and the way out of suffering. They, on the basis of their own long and sincere search, immedi-ately understood and knew that this was indeed a Buddha, an Enlightened One, and they became his first disciples.

Siddhartha Gautama, now the Buddha, went on from

there to teach constantly until he died at just over eighty years of age. Some people followed and heard him for most of their lives, yet never really understood his words, while others, on hearing the teaching once from the Buddha or from an enlightened disciple, were instantly able to fully comprehend the meaning and so became enlightened. They are called arahats (in Sanskrit) or arahants (in Pali). The Buddha accepted all who came, from kings and Brahmins and wandering ascetics to householders and Sudras. And he accepted women also.

WHAT DID HE LOOK LIKE?

It is said in ancient records that the Buddha had blue eyes. This is not at all unlikely in view of the area where he was born, where blue eyes are not uncommon. Another record, said to be his own reply to a question put to him by a Brahmin, says he was six feet tall. The translation into English used the word 'fathom', which is, of course, a measurement of six feet. In other records he is said to have had a serene, compassionate expression and it is said that he often smiled. There are even some records of him rebuking certain disciples, so he was not a soft or inspid teacher. These records are from *Thus Have I Heard: Long Discourses of the Buddha (The Digha Nikāya)*.

As well as these quite believable descriptions of the Buddha, there are others—such as the story of his having hair in which every curl turned in one direction; certain descriptions of his genitalia; accounts of webbing between his digits; and imprints of the wheel of life on the soles of his feet. These are pre-Buddhist beliefs said to be the marks of the superior man. These accounts came into the stream of Buddhist teachings, holus-bolus, brought in by Brahmin followers in later times, and are purported to have arisen from the Buddha's agreement with questions put to him by a Brahmin.

One particular mark of the superior man is more easily understood: the elongated ear lobes. This is another pre-Buddhist belief and is found in other places in the world. It comes from the fact that, in certain cultures, the rich wore heavy earrings and the richer (and therefore heavier) the ornaments, the more they stretched the wearer's ear lobes. It is quite probable the Buddha in his 'domestic' life wore ornate earrings, but records indicate he did not do so after setting out on his quest for enlightenment and did, in fact, discourage this practice in his disciples once they became what we call monks and nuns.

FROM PRINCE TO PAUPER: WHY?

Why did the Buddha—young, healthy, fortunate in social position; confident of his future prospects; and sure of every pleasure life could offer—simply walk away from it all? Part of the answer lay in his character: he was a deep thinker all his life; part lay in custom: the practice of leaving home to become a seeker-after-knowledge; and part, perhaps the greater part, lay in his acute awareness of the lack of lasting satisfaction in life and the resultant suffering of sentient beings who did not understand the cause of their suffering. If he could find the causes of this suffering and its cure, he could share his knowledge with all who would listen. Perhaps someone

else had already made the discovery! This is why he spent
more than six years seeking the wisdom of those who
were supposed to be the wisest men of his time and
country. They all had ideas of how to achieve such
knowledge but so far none had found it. Enlightenment
was not a matter of angelic messengers nor of godly
voices; it was something one had to find for oneself—
and it still is.

THE BASIC TEACHINGS

What are the *basic* teachings of Buddhism? Put very briefly,
they are commonly expressed as suffering (dukha),
impermanence (anicca) and no-self (anatta). Suffering.
Impermanence. Emptiness.

The most basic Buddhist beliefs and the most important were the Four Noble Truths and the Eightfold Path.
This is where the uselessness of words as means of explanation becomes obvious. Whole volumes could be and,
in fact, have been written on every word of the Buddha
as memorised by his Sangha (company of monks and
nuns) and written down soon after his death. (Possibly
some of them were written down in his lifetime and lost.)
All these words are necessary, helpful signposts. They
vary because of the variety of human understanding and
expression, which is why he did not encourage the
written record, regarding vocal repetition by groups as
being more reliable. Once the *core* of the philosophy is
realised by the seeker, these written records are no longer
useful, because the journey then becomes an inner one
of personal experience.

Rather than simply list the Four Noble Truths and the

Eightfold Path, I will add a few words of clarification,
words based on the thoughts of wiser heads than mine.

The Four Noble Truths
1. There is dukha. This term is incorrectly translated
   simply as suffering, but it really has something of the
   meaning of lacking in *lasting* satisfaction. Within this
   truth also lies the philosophy of impermanence of all
   dependently arisen phenomena.
2. The reason for dukha is craving or 'thirst'—
   desirousness.
3. There *is* a way out of dukha and suffering.
4. The way out of dukha is the Eightfold Path.

Dukha takes in all the unhappiness to which the flesh
and spirit are heir; unhappiness caused by craving for
what we think will bring us happiness and free us from
unhappiness. All life, from the single cell on, seeks to be
safe and comfortable rather than remain in discomfort.
When we find what seems to bring us happiness, we
cling to it and crave more of the same. We do not understand impermanence. Absolutely nothing remains the
same for as long as a snap of the fingers. We cannot really
accept this fact and we equate it with suffering. Although
the impermanence of 'happy' phenomena seems to us a
tragedy, we fail to accept that impermanence also applies
to 'unhappiness'.

All of Buddha's teachings offer layers of meaning,
depending how far the student wishes to go or is capable
of understanding. What I write here is, as I have previously stated, basic, down-to-earth, non-mystical Buddhism. Those who want a deeper understanding will find
it. This is simply an effort to show the non-practitioner

what lies behind the beliefs of the people belonging to a group 500-million-strong around the world, many of whom are now part of the Australian population.

For the practising Buddhist, both lay and Sangha, part of the way to live a happier life is to follow the Eightfold Path.

The Eightfold Path

In order to follow this path we are advised to cultivate:

1. Right views or understanding free from superstition.
2. Right aims, high and worthy of the intelligent, earnest person.
3. Right speech, kindly, open, truthful.
4. Right conduct in all concerns of life.
5. Right livelihood, doing no harm to sentient beings.
6. Right perseverance in all the other seven steps.
7. Right mindfulness, the ever watchful, attentive mind.
8. Right contemplation, earnest thought on the deep mysteries of life.

There are many translations of the Eightfold Path, some differing slightly in wording from the list above, but to all Buddhists the essence is the same.

KARMA, REINCARNATION, REBIRTH

Certain words and phrases in connection with Buddhist *religion* are most used but least understood by the uninformed or those who have accepted them without analysis, or simply out of respect for the one who taught. This acceptance out of respect for the teacher is absolutely contrary to the Dharma.

The Buddha taught his followers not to believe even what he said out of respect for him, but to investigate it for themselves. If one does this, that is, listens carefully to what is taught, with respect for the greater wisdom of others, then pulls everything that has been taught or that one has studied into tiny bits to analyse it, the conclusion to accept or reject the teaching is as close as we can get, as individuals, to what is 'truth'. It follows that any truth, at any given time, may not be your truth, and there is nothing permanent about any truth. What has been accepted as absolute truth at one time has been utterly refuted at another.

The three words—karma, reincarnation and rebirth—although having different meanings, are so entwined in the average Buddhist and non-Buddhist mind that they must be considered in their interconnectedness.

Karma means action. This definition, which Buddha used, means, to begin with, cause and effect. For example, if you waste your money, you will experience the result, which is debt and poverty; if you are careless with guns and sharp instruments, you will harm yourself and others; if you insult someone grievously, you will have lost a friend or made an enemy; if excessive rain falls in a catchment area, there will be flooding. Simple cause and effect.

Of course, karma is more than a case of 'I do this and that happens', because there is much more going on in existence than what 'you' do. All phenomena are compound. What goes on in one place affects what goes on in another, no matter how minute in effect. We seem to forget the words of the old pop song, 'The foot bone's connected to the leg bone'.

So that is karma. If your religion teaches reincarnation

of the individual self, as pre- and non-Buddhist Indian and Asian religions did (and as most religious groups, including Christian, did in one way or another through history), it seems evident to most believers that, when one reincarnates, there will be debts to pay and delayed rewards to receive. Then—hey presto!—to the mind, karma (action/reaction) becomes Karma (punishment and reward—heaven or hell in the new existence). Buddha taught karma—a natural non-judgmental action and reaction—not Karma. Sad as it is to have to say it, *I* probably was *not* an ancient Egyptian princess or a famous medieval courtesan in a past life. Others may have been if they think so. I simply have no such 'past life' memories. Nevertheless, I did say I have a 'rational' type mind, which some may consider dull.

Rebirth is a word most often used by people who mistake it to mean reincarnation. It's a natural misunderstanding coming from lack of reflection. One view of rebirth points to nature and the seasons: what 'dies' in one season is 'reborn' in another. The elements of the physical body 'die' and are reborn as trees and grass and flowers. The energy of 'mind' or 'soul' or 'spirit' leaves one plane of existence and comes into being again or proceeds to another plane.

Buddha never argued as to whether or not there is something more after death. He taught the Dharma of no-self and put the question: as there is no inherent, permanent self, only a constantly changing physical, emotional or philosophical state, what is reborn? When asking questions of this nature, he would often point to a shady tree and suggest the listener sit in the shade and think about the question from every angle, or, to put it another way, meditate on it. The outcome of your deliberations and mine may not be in full agreement, but then, your experiences have been different from mine. It is well to remember here that what we call death is a momentary phenomenon—not an end, but part of ongoing existence. There is no actual *moment* of death as such—no *moment* that is an *end*.

METTA, KARUNA, LOVING KINDNESS, COMPASSION

Becoming a follower of the Buddha's way and studying the Dharma is meant to develop sympathetic under-standing, gentleness and the ability to see the reasons for another's behaviour. If one did no more than act with real compassion in every situation, one would almost be a Buddha. The sincere practice of universal compassion in life cannot avoid leading to enlighten-ment. The mind set on this path will seek to see clearly what needs to be done—or not done—and the best and most compassionate way to go about it. And seeing *clearly* is the name of the game.

Metta, karuna and compassion, do not mean that one needs to throw one's arms around a Hitler, a child molester or a rapist. It does mean that we remain aware that here too is a sentient being suffering hor-ribly from ignorance. Weeping over him or her won't help anyone and it may not be our place to have any-thing physical to do with the matter. Yet even while keeping our distance from the 'criminal', we still acknowledge that he or she and all sentient beings experienc. suffering. We keep our do-gooding for where it will do good.

TO BECOME A BUDDHIST

What does one do to become a Buddhist? Is there a ceremony like baptism or 'witnessing'? Primarily, of course, there has to be the desire to 'seek Refuge', which implies *some* knowledge of what one is letting oneself in for (that is, unless the person is simply following in the footsteps of their parents, or the desire stems from a person's cultural background—not uncommon reasons for being a Buddhist). One goes to a member of the Sangha, of whatever sect of Buddhism one has chosen, and asks to be given Refuge. There may be others with you or you may be the sole candidate. The Refuge vows and Five Precepts will be explained. If you accept all the explanations, a ceremony will be arranged. It is customary to make offerings to defray the costs, but no genuine candidate would be refused if they were too poor to do this.

The ceremony takes place in the temple but this is not absolutely mandatory. It may be simple or quite elaborate, depending on cultural convention. Three times one states that one goes for Refuge to the Buddha, the Dharma and the Sangha. Then one is given the Five Precepts by which one, as a lay Buddhist, will attempt to live one's life.

THE FIVE BUDDHIST PRECEPTS

1. No lying.
2. No stealing or taking what is not offered.
3. No killing.
4. No unlawful or unnatural sexual activity.

5. No intoxication (by drugs, drink etc.), which dulls the mind and makes one foolish.

There are three further precepts taken for one day at a time over certain intervals:

1. To eat only one meal per day and that to be finished by noon.
2. Not to sleep on high beds (this means to deny oneself ease and luxury).
3. No sexual activity.

Monks and nuns make vows additional to these. On becoming Buddhist one may, or may not, conform to the cultural pattern of a certain sect, depending on how relevant one feels it to be to one's journey towards enlightenment. Study and meditation go without saying.

The Buddha advised his followers to choose their friends carefully and to not waste precious time on unsuitable companions. There is no point in spending time with people who turn every discussion into an argument. Contributing to their feelings of aggression is hardly practising loving kindness.

Buddha was most unpopular with the Brahmin caste when he taught the unnecessary cruelty of blood sacrifices. The general populace spent heavily on the purchase of animals and fowls, and the priests' fees so that the animals could be slaughtered and the omens read by the priests who were the only ones with the 'power' to do so. The temples literally ran with blood in those days. By rejecting the practice, the Buddha's teaching appeared to jeopardise the excessive incomes of the priests.

There are no 'priests' in Buddhism, although nowadays monks and nuns do carry out rituals that can be performed only by them and which, in the non-Buddhist view, come so close to the duties of priests and priestesses they are indistinguishable from them.

DEATH AND DYING

Regarding the Buddhist view of death and dying, it may be said (with no flippancy intended) that the Tibetans are the 'experts' in this field. The reason for this is cultural as well as religious. Broadly speaking, Buddhism accepts that none of us knows the exact hour of our death, not even if we have been sentenced to death judicially or if we are terminally ill. Most of us deliberately or subconsciously ignore the subject of death altogether, although friends, relatives and strangers are dying around us at every moment. Death seems to be some strange but quite natural phenomenon that will and does happen to 'other' people—not to us. Others see death as the only way out of unhappiness and suffering.

For most of us the fear is not primarily of death per se, because common sense tells us we can't avoid it no matter how hard we 'fight' it, but of the *manner* of our death. Will we die alone and lonely, or in dreadful pain with loss of all dignity? Will we be so afraid that our dying hours become hours of terror, fearful of what is seen as approaching annihilation of the self? It is the *dying*, not the death everyone worries about, whether they expect there to be heaven 'on the other side' or not.

The Buddhist attitude is that, in order to have a peaceful death, we need to practise having a peaceful life, to live each day as though it were the last. Leave no animosity, resentment, vengeful thoughts, unpaid emotional debts, disturbing regrets or unresolved misunderstandings at the day's end. Behave as though Karma (reward and punishment) really is a part of the after-death experience and be prepared. In this way the mind will be calm and peaceful at all times, even if death comes much sooner than expected.

The other side of this practice is that, with a calm and peaceful attitude toward death and dying, we can be of great help to those who *are* dying now and who know it. This may all sound very depressing, but look at the Buddhists you may know. Are they perpetually miserable and gloomy? Not at all. By being prepared for death, one has done away with humanity's greatest fear and left oneself able to be of help to others at *their* time of greatest need. And then one can get on with whatever living one has left.

NO SELF? NO ME?

The Buddhist teaching that gives most people, even members of the Sangha, the greatest puzzlement is the doctrine of no-self. This has to be taught according to the capacity of the listener to understand. It is not recommended that it is taught indiscriminately, as it can have a deep psychological effect on a mind that is not well balanced and on the hearer who does not listen carefully enough. The simplest way to explain the doctrine of no-self is as follows. We think of ourselves as permanent and existing inherently. Due to the impermanence of all compound phenomena, this cannot be so. Everything is

changing all the time and that includes every cell of our
bodies, all our emotions, our attitudes and opinions. This
'self' is not as we are accustomed to seeing it—eternal
and unchanging—but then, neither is anything else.

To talk on this subject to people with low self-esteem
often gives them the idea that what is meant is that they
are 'no-one' or 'nothing'. That is not at all what is meant.
It is an illustration of the illusion in which we pass our
lives; we assume 'things' exist inherently on the basis of
our limited means of perception. An example might be
love or hate at first sight. The object of the emotion
appears to us to be this or that—desirable or disgusting.
The truth may be so, may not be so, may be the other
way around, or something in between, yet we are quite
sure we are absolutely correct in our estimation of the
situation. Then, when what is desirable seems to change
into something disgusting we are devastated, and later,
possibly, surprised when what we had thought of as disgusting turns out to be nothing of the sort. It was all
illusion. This goes on with us all the time—day in, day
out—confusion heaped on confusion. From it come
broken friendships, parent–child rifts, romantic tragedies,
unhappiness and suffering for all, brought about by reluctance to take into account as much as possible in a given
situation before acting, be it out of attachment or anger.
To die in such mental confusion would be dreadful.
Therefore, it behoves us—in modern parlance—to clean
up our act as soon as possible and to begin to enjoy all
the living we have left to do.

There are no 'thou shalts' in Buddhism, only an invi-
tation to investigate for oneself; no 'sinners' and 'saved',
only the ignorant and the enlightened. The problem is
ignorance—of what is, and is not, skilful behaviour.

Skilful behaviour (that is, considered behaviour based on as much information and contemplation as possible) leads to peace of mind and happiness, and unskilful behaviour leads to confusion and misery. Buddha wanted to help all sentient beings to find happiness in the here and now.

WHO FOLLOWED THE BUDDHA?

The caste system had come into force before the days of the Buddha and it was taken very seriously indeed by members of the Brahmin caste, whose religious texts, the Vedas, state that if a sudra speaks about the 'scriptures' his tongue shall be split and if he as much as listens, his ears are to be filled with molten lead. However, the Buddha made no distinctions based on caste lines or on other types of discrimination. He spoke to anyone or any group coming to hear what he had to say.

After he had instructed his first disciples and was satisfied that they understood what he had told them, he sent them out to repeat the teaching. Buddha then became, by word of mouth, a much sought-after teacher. Reigning kings (rajahs and maharajahs) sought him out for personal and practical as well as philosphical advice. He was, due to his previous social standing, welcome in palaces and amongst the well educated, but his more general teachings usually took place in the open, so that an unrestricted audience might gather.

There was never anything in his teachings that inflamed his listeners or led to riotous behaviour, so rulers and wealthy people offered him parks and groves in their own domains for use as meeting places and retreat centres. These times of retreat were held during the rainy season, when foot travel was almost impossible and often dangerous. To this day, Buddhist monks and nuns, as well as many lay people, hold the Rains Retreat between May and August—full-time if possible. For those in monasteries this is easy, but for self-supporting Western Buddhist Sangha members in the day-to-day workforce, participating in a full-time retreat can be disappointingly difficult. One can only do one's best in this regard.

FAITH AND BELIEF

Buddhism does not teach blind faith or belief. What is required is seeing existence as clearly as we can, and being as free of our concepts and misperceptions as possible. Yet one is not expected to be fanatically attached to 'truth', as one sees it, or to any stage on the journey toward enlightenment. Buddha often used parables. They helped his listeners to understand him and the parable of the raft is still a favourite. Buddha likened his teachings to a raft constructed for the safe crossing of troubled waters. Once across the stream, it would be pointless to hoist the raft onto one's back and continue clinging to it on that safe shore. Much better to leave it for those who might be able to use it. The one who has already crossed the stream (that is, has fully understood the Dharma) no longer needs the raft, because it has fulfilled its purpose.

QUESTIONING THE BUDDHA

During his teaching life, which spanned more than forty-five years, Buddha was perpetually questioned by those seeking knowledge as well as by those trying to refute his philosophy. He consistently refused to contend with his questioners on any subject of a metaphysical nature. He neither agreed nor disagreed, telling such questioners that imaginative speculation on certain subjects was useless.

One such questioner was his own disciple, Malinkyaputta, who, realising that many of the problems he had repeatedly put to the Buddha had been put aside without explanation, decided at last to demand clarification. His problems were ten in number:

1. Is the universe eternal? or
2. Is it not eternal?
3. Is the universe finite? or
4. Is it infinite?
5. Is the 'soul' (ātman or spirit) the same as the body? or
6. Is the soul one thing and the body another?
7. Does the Tathagata (another term used for an enlightened teacher) exist after death? or
8. Does he not exist after death?
9. Does he both (simultaneously) not exist or exist after death? or
10. Does he both (simultaneously) not exist and not not exist?

Malinkyaputta obviously spent much time thinking but not about matters of most importance in his own search for clarity.

The Buddha asked the disciple if he had ever said to him: 'Come and lead the holy life under me, I will explain these questions to you.' He also asked if Malinkyaputta had ever said to him: 'Sir, I will lead the holy life under the Blessed One and he will explain these questions to me.' Buddha said that if anyone refused to lead the holy life under him until tnese questions were explained, that person would die with the questions unanswered. Then he told Malinkyaputta the following parable:

> Suppose a man is wounded by a poison arrow and is brought to the doctor. Now suppose the man refuses to be treated until he knows who shot him; whether he is a member of this or that class; what his name and family might be; whether he is short or tall or of medium height; whether his complexion is black, brown or golden; which town or village he comes from. Suppose the sick man says he will not be treated until he knows the kind of bow with which he was shot; the kind of bowstring used; the type of arrow; what sort of feather was on the arrow; and what sort of material the point of the arrow was made of.

Buddha explained that the man would die before he could know the answers to those questions and he explained to Malinkyaputta that whatever *opinion* one might have about the questions asked, there still remained the problems of birth, old age, decay, death, sorrow, lamentation, pain, grief and distress—the cessation of which Buddha *had* explained. To explain these matters, he said, was useful and helpful to aversion (to unskilful behaviour), non-attachment, tranquillity and full realisation. This seemed to set Malinkyaputta on a new train of thought, because elsewhere he is reported to have approached the Buddha for further instruction and, later on, to have become enlightened.

THE BEGINNINGS OF THE MONASTIC MOVEMENT

With the passing of the years the number of Buddha's followers increased rapidly. Most were people who flocked to hear him whenever he was in their area, but there were also others who wished to be with him at all times, wanting more instruction than they could get from an occasional talk. Still others followed because the Buddha was fast becoming the most talked-about of teachers and to be his follower was the 'in' thing to be. Time weeded out most of these, but not all. Then there were those who wished to devote their lives to learning all they could from the Teacher; beginning with those first five ascetics, they became the first members of the Sangha.

Not only men wished to hear the Buddha's words. Queens and courtesans, wealthy women, housewives and young unwed girls all came to hear this new wisdom. They made offerings of food and land and invited the Teacher and his chief disciples into their homes. Buddha made no distinction between the men and the women. He spoke in exactly the same way to all.

There has developed an idea, mainly in Western society and the feminist movement, that Buddha discriminated *against* women, that he did not approve of women in some way. This is not so and there are records of his praise for the intelligence of certain women and their complete grasp of what he was teaching. I will enlarge on this subject in a further section dealing with Buddhist monasticism.

NO COMMANDMENTS

It is commonly thought that to be a Buddhist also means to be a strict vegetarian. Not so. The reason behind vegetarianism in Buddhist religious practice is the precept not to kill. The original idea behind this precept was that all life is sacred and therefore to kill animals and birds for religious sacrifice was cruel and unnecessary. There was no pity or compassion for the slaughtered sacrificial creatures.

Precepts are not commandments. There are no 'thou shalt nots' in Buddhism. If there is anything close to a commandment it is this: THINK. Think about what you are doing, why you are doing it and what could be some of the most likely outcomes. In this respect, Buddhists attempt to act skilfully rather than unskilfully and to avoid extremes of behaviour. They attempt to follow the Middle Way.

MEAT OR VEG?

Naturally, one can do only the best one can. In countries where the climate permits the easy growing of fruits and vegetables, vegetarianism is easy. Where extensive raising of vegetables for food is not part of the culture, such as in Tibet and Mongolia, meat is a necessary part of the diet. In China and Japan, fish and soy-bean products provide necessary protein. Fowl, eggs and fish do this in some other cultures. Originally, the monks and nuns took their begging bowls into the town or the village in the morning, where the people each gave a little of what they could. This was then taken back to the group and shared as the one meal of the day, eaten just before noon.

The earliest Buddhist teaching on this subject, said to be Buddha's own teaching, was to accept what was offered, be thankful for it, but not to ask that anything be killed for *you*. This makes sense, for if the 'beggars' inspected the contents of their bowls and picked out and rejected what they did not fancy, those who had gladly offered what they could would not feel encouraged to continue the practice.

If it should be necessary to kill to eat, the Buddhist does so with compassion. Thanking the bird or animal sharpens the awareness that the creature is a suffering sentient being, just as the Buddhist is. Responsibility for one's actions *always* lies with oneself in Buddhism.

In the monasteries today, and for those laypersons undertaking a full day's eight precepts, the practice is to eat the main meal before noon and then take only fluids until the next morning, when breakfast may or may not be eaten, according to the rules of the particular monastery. A strict search of larger establishments would, no doubt, reveal many a small cache of 'nibbles' in robe cupboards or such places. This is least likely in a Zen monastery. I am not a real Mother Hubbard, my cupboard seldom being totally bare.

NEAR THE END

After forty-five years of travelling and teaching, the Sage of the Sakya clan, as Buddha became known, was (compared with the expected lifespan in India then) a very old man. His strength was failing at last and his faithful attendant Ananda did all he could for his Teacher's health and comfort. It was in Kusinara that the Buddha died, surrounded by many of his Sangha members and followers. His body was cremated and his ashes were divided to be interred in shrines around the country. Later they were re-divided and further dispersed.

In the late nineteenth century, an urn bearing this inscription was found at Piprahwa in India:

> This is the urn of the relics of the
> Bhagavat, the Buddha of the Sakya tribe,
> that is enshrined (by honourable brothers
> and sisters, wives and children).

> Kogen Mizuno, *The Beginnings of Buddhism*

The title 'Bhagavat' means a sage. 'The Buddha of the Sakya tribe' was the title used of Siddhartha Gautama during and after his lifetime. The urn is accepted as having, in all probability, been the family share of the relics.

❧

2

THE RELEVANCE OF
BUDDHISM HERE
AND NOW

*What do ordinary Buddhists believe and
practise?*

❧

What exactly (or as nearly as possible) is the definition of what we call Buddhism? It is popularly
known, even to most of its adherents, as a religion. That
being the case, what exactly (or as nearly as possible) is
the definition of a religion?

According to *Webster's Dictionary*, a religion is 'the
service or adoration of God as expressed in forms of
worship, in obedience to divine commandments and in
pursuit of a way of life'. *Odham's Dictionary* defines
religion as 'the belief in a supernatural power or powers,
belief in a god or gods, especially such belief as entails

acts of worship on the part of the believer; a developed system of philosphical, theological and ethical opinions, tenets and theories depending ultimately and essentially upon a belief in a deity or deities, and the necessity of worshipping that deity or those deities . . .'

According to these definitions, it is understandable that popular Buddhism is seen as a religion and that the Buddha is clung to out of misplaced devotion and super-stition. However, Buddhism does not teach that Buddha is God or even *a* god; the Buddha gave no command-ments regarding service to or worship of himself; he was not, and did not claim to be, supernatural; he was a human being whose only difference to the human beings of today was cultural, and even that has not changed greatly in the area in which he lived. Basic human nature and inherited beliefs do not always keep pace with advancing technology.

So is Buddhism a religion? Yes and no. Yes—devotion to the memory of the Buddha in different cultural envi-ronments has brought a 'Buddhist' religion into being. No—basic Buddhism is a philosophy of morality and ethics, and much more. Buddhism is not a religion unless, because of one's needs, one wishes to make it so.

Of what possible relevance to modern society are the philosophical–ethical–moral teachings of a man who was born 2,500 years ago? With the abundance—even over-abundance—of differing religions in the world today, what can Buddhism offer? With the wonders of the modern media deluging us with recipes for both mental and physical self-improvement, and offering this, that and the other type of therapy—self-applied or 'professional'—what is it about this ancient philosophy that even today draws people of different

lack of lasting satisfaction

races and nationalities in their thousands?

The answer is simply that, in spite of almost magical technological advances, there is still dukha. Everyone still experiences birth, old age, sickness, death, association with unpleasant persons and conditions, separation from loved ones and pleasant conditions, not getting what one desires, grief, lamentation and other forms of mental and physical suffering. These are all included in the word dukha. No-one escapes it. Dukha is what existence is all about and each of us has to find a way to handle it with the least possible trauma. This search is called 'the pursuit of happiness'.

The international news for just one day is enough to show that most of humanity's solutions to suffering do not work and more often than not leave the original problem worse, while creating a few more to keep it company. There are a thousand grisly stories of efforts to do good going wrong. We do not see clearly the inter-connectedness of phenomena. There is an old saying that in doing good to someone 'evil' one may be doing evil to someone 'good'. And 'fools rush in where angels fear to tread' (without thinking clearly about the eventual outcome of their actions). We read it in daily papers, hear it on radio and watch it on television. I can think of no worse way to start the day than to listen to the inter-national or even local news. Our adrenalin output goes up and then it crashes. Result: a feeling of hopeless depression. But not for all of us? No. Some have strongly developed 'Pollyanna' characteristics, always cheerful, heads full of dreams (nothing wrong with that), seeking always to assess a given situation and mentally transform-ing the deficits into something easier to handle. Yet not even Pollyannas can avoid the other half of the picture, and often the bright optimism is a shield against panic, despair, and the fear of giving in and of being over-whelmed emotionally.

Established religions are losing followers from among the educated. Many have lost faith in 'faith' and faiths. There is nothing unfortunate in this except that few of the doubters and 'disbelievers' have found anything that works better for them. Unfortunately, there is no instant, universal cure for the problem, for the very obvious reason that, even with all our similiarities and intercon-nectedness, we are still individual bundles of energy with different psychological patterns, forever bumping up against one another, sometimes causing pleasure and sometimes causing severe irritation to everyone around us.

With the progress of education and learning across the world today, the numbers of doubters, unbelievers, seekers after enlightenment and the spiritually empty will increase. Where does one turn for something that makes sense? Something that helps us to get the most out of life?

The appeal of Buddhism has not waned after many years of development. The basic, original philosophy remains as always, but the *religious* side of Buddhism has developed because of the needs of those whose psycho-logical and emotional make-up leads them in another direction. It is probably due to this diversion of ways that Buddhism is still expanding today.

The moral and ethical side of Buddhism covers both the philosophical as well as the more specifically relig-ious aspects and what holds for the religious devotee holds equally for the philosophical seeker. The moral–ethical principles, which are not commandments but advice, are embodied in the Five Precepts. The lack of commandments in the Buddha's teachings arises from the doctrine that we are each ultimately responsible for our own karma—*the results of our own mental, physical and verbal behaviour.* The old excuse that he or she *made* me do it, that is, lose my temper, feel sad or happy and so on, just does not wash for a Buddhist. Regular analytical meditation is needed to keep this prominently in the forefront of the mind—constant *mindfulness.* Easy? Of course not. Whatever is worth possessing requires effort.

While morals and ethics appear to be of decreasing importance to more and more people today, society can only make more ad hoc laws in an attempt to force its citizens to act responsibly for their own sakes as well as for the sake of society as a whole. All that this achieves is more crime, because there are more laws to be broken, more actions forbidden. Forbidding people to act in certain ways hasn't worked since Adam and Eve were young and ate the fruit of a particular tree. We know how they responded to the injunction not to eat the fruit. They took a calculated risk and ate it, as more and more people do today.

The more we stress the 'rights' of the individual over the 'rights' of society as a whole, the less awesome seems the law to the individual and the less respect the individual feels for the authority of society. If the laws stand in the way of individuals' perceived pleasures, then their wishes become of greater importance. In an ideal society wishes versus laws might work well and the need for laws would finally wither away. Another situation could be where everyone accepted responsibility for their actions as well as the outcomes (karma), instead of expecting to be pulled out of self-made difficulties by friends, relatives or the authority they (often rightly)

despise. Whichever way it goes is not conducive to hap-
pinesss. An ideal society remains an *ideal* only. Personal
freedom also means personal responsibility.

So here we are, stuck in a mess that seems to get pro-
gressively messier. What to do? Where to start? The Buddhist reply is to start right *here*, right *now* and begin to
study mind control. Your mind. My mind. Not brain-
washing, which is control by outside forces, but from
within oneself.

Begin with the Four Noble Truths. All the help we
need to begin is in the first two Noble Truths, could we
but see it clearly.

The **First Noble Truth**, or Truth of the Nobles as it
should be translated, states that life is dukha. It seems
obvious, especially the longer one lives, and yet most
people in every new generation never consider this.
Never. They talk about their particular 'luck' and 'fate' and
'Karma', and genetics and nurture, but they can't see that
it is the same for everyone else. To acknowledge the
natural existence of dukha undermines self-pity. Dukha
isn't just *my* fate, it is *everyone's* fate. No-one escapes.
The most saintly do-gooder experiences dukha. The
richest human being in the world cannot possibly escape
it, nor the poorest. The healthiest creature born and living
in the most ideal conditions is still subject to dukha. In
the *religion* of Buddhism, even the 'gods' are subject to
dukha. The first stop on the path to release from dukha
is to become truly aware of it. Don't hide from the truth
and pretend it isn't so. No-one can cure a condition like
this unless they acknowledge it. An alcoholic cannot be
cured unless they admit the problem. The same applies
to a drug addict or a person suffering from tuberculosis
or sexually transmitted diseases.

Step two on the path to release from dukha is the *wish* to be free of suffering. I say 'free from suffering' because dukha is not all bad. Impermanence, or change that alters a preferred situation, also alters the ones we would like to escape. But it doesn't happen in a nice orderly pattern of ups and downs. There are multitudes of patterns developing and declining in an interconnected manner all the time. For the person with no conception of dukha (real life) the result is ignorance (of reality), confusion, frustration, and quite often some degree of moral or mental 'breakdown'. One would imagine there would be few intelligent beings who would *not* wish to be free of such a condiiton, but there are millions, if not billions. Even though we see others who appear to have accepted life as it is and are acting accordingly, many do not ask themselves why this is so. They see only their own condition. Life seems so 'unfair'. Why do *they* deserve this cruel fate? Why should *some* people have everything? What is the reason for it all?

The **Second Noble Truth** states that dukha arises through craving and clinging. This is not the same as wanting something possible or needful; it is the craving, the desire for the impossible, or what is impossible for us as particular individuals. Who on a limited income doesn't sometimes desire the wealth of an Aga Khan? What plain-featured man or woman does not desire a beautiful face? It is sensible to want what we need, but it is a source of suffering to crave the unattainable. All the craving in the world would not have given the man who was the Aga Khan his gold. He was born to that position and it was then his 'fate' to receive his weight in gold on special birthdays. He, no doubt, craved things quite other than gold.

It is a misunderstanding of this particular dharma that

gives rise to the assumption that a Buddhist should *want* nothing at all and should spend all their time under a tree 'navel-gazing'; in other words, that a Buddhist should not live a normal life in the world into which they are born. The Buddha did not confine his compassion to ascetics only, and even they, once they understood his teaching, went out to teach others rather than continue their fruitless ascetic practices. He taught kings and business people, householders and artisans, and gave advice according to their best interests. He never told those people to give all their belongings away and spend their lives listening only to what he had to say.

The Buddha liked to get to the root of whatever the problem might be. His aim was to show the sufferer, or the seeker after enlightenment, the solution, not to prove to his listeners how metaphysically obscure he could be. When trying to solve our individual problems, we too need to get right down to basics. The basis of society's problems lies within each individual. Each can do something about the whole problem but not everything. No one person can 'save the planet'.

The place to begin is at the individual level. When we work at solving our own problems we have already made a contribution to solving the problems around us. Most of us don't really want to become fully enlightened, it seems too difficult to achieve. Nevertheless we can *lessen* the effects of our dukha. If we see the Buddhist method working, we can use it. No-one needs to become a Buddhist to use the Buddha's teachings for personal benefit.

Whose Fault Is It?
It has become customary to blame our shortcomings on any number of outside influences, some of which are the

conditions of our birth and parental care, our nurture, our environment and how other people behave toward us. Disapproval of any of these assumed sources of our troubles is no solution, even where the responsibility, or part of it, can be correctly placed. The matter of who or what is responsible is of secondary importance. The matter of first importance is to see the problem as it is now, as clearly as possible. Look into all the hows and whys that brought the problem into being. Don't deny our own part in it, because we do have some responsibility for what happens to us. Some call it Karma and trace responsibility back through countless past lives, sometimes going beyond the Middle Way into extremes of metaphysical fantasy: for example, the Karmic reason E was born with no arms was because she cut off someone's arms in a previous incarnation. Not thalidomide? No. E probably did something very bad to her mother in a previous life and the mother's taking thalidomide is said to be the Karma of that situation.

This is *not* Buddhist teaching at all. While their belief in Karma may cause some people to behave well, how much better it would be if they understood karma (with a small k) well and behaved accordingly.

If it is true that people believe only what they want to believe, then the world is full of those who prefer suffering. Yet there is such a simple remedy for beginning the healing process:

Enjoy what you have now but accept that it is already changing.
Do no harm to living beings, including yourself.
Learn to control your mind by striving to see things as they really are, now.

At the risk of preaching to the already converted, there is always the hope that there are people who are still receptive to new ideas and new ways to view situations, or people who have become so desperate for a 'cure' for their condition that they will go so far as to acitively *seek* a cure. Like the sixth century Buddhist patriarch Hui Neng, they may be in a suitable mental (spiritual) state to comprehend the Buddha's teachings from a few words unintentionally overheard or a few words read—perhaps even in this book.

People cannot be forced to *believe* something, not even if they are taught doctrine by rote. This applies especially to Buddhist philosophy, where belief depends on personal experience. We can talk to someone about a delightful or horrifying experience and describe it minutely, but the hearer will never fully understand or be able to *believe* what they are told unless they have the opportunity to assess the matter as fully as possible for themselves. We cannot truly ever know exactly what another person is feeling, even though we may have had very similar experiences. Being in a small boat at sea in a hurricane can be brilliantly described, losing a loved one to a lingering illness can be discussed, the safe birth of a longed-for child can be talked about, but no-one can know what any of these experiences is really like unless and until they *experience* the same or a very similar condition. True understanding and *real* belief can come only from personal *experience*. Buddhism is a *personal* experience.

Craving

The cause of dukha (craving) is not *wanting*, nor is it simply *needing*. Craving, as it is used here, is the permanent condition of *desirousness*. It is our wish to possess wholly, to cling to. When we desire or crave to have something, we want it to remain as it is at that moment. We want to be able to *have* our cake as well as enjoy eating it; we want the person we 'love' never to change; we want death to be suspended where we and our families are concerned. In other more topical words, we want the good times to roll and roll and roll . . . We cannot accept that other Buddhist teaching: impermanence (anicca). Yet compound phenomena are subject to change. The body I was born with is not the body I drag about today. The river I step into this morning will not be the same river this evening—nor even one second from now.

The clinging, the craving, the expectation of permanence is the cause of suffering. Clinging to concepts and opinions is a cause of violence and suffering. We try to put ourselves in the right by speaking about our 'principles', which we will kill or die for. Often the 'principles' are badly flawed, but we will never admit that possibility. Anyone who has different 'principles' becomes, automatically, 'the enemy'. We will stand by our principles to the death—the death, preferably, of the 'others'.

We find the perfect partner and life is sweet, satisfying (sukha). The partner changes (for a variety of reasons) and we are in hell on earth, quite forgetting that we too have changed. Parents delight in the babyhood of their child. They think they know all there is to know about this person and suffer greatly as the child changes, disagrees with them and one day gladly leaves them.

We may live in a place where we have known only happiness and a feeling of security, only to be suddenly uprooted because of economic or environmental changes. We may even lose our small treasures because of, for example, flood or fire, and, at the same time, we may lose a loved one. We may still, after all is gone, mentally cling to our memories of past events as something concrete and real, and so prolong our grief.

Nothing can make us leap for joy in the face of sorrow, but if, to begin with, we are aware of impermanence, we halve the pain. We learn that craving and clinging are the cause of the pain, more than the loss itself.

How often we add to the sadness of a dying loved one by clinging to them, refusing to face the impermanence of life, refusing to allow the one near death to speak about their feelings. Facing facts and gently letting go, no matter how painful to the survivors, often makes for an easier death. When our own time to die comes, letting go is the more sensible, more dignified way to go than raging against the inevitable, like a child fighting against being weaned.

The most damaging part of craving and clinging can be that they preclude investigation or analysis of a situation, preclude our seeing things as they really are (or as near as possible, given our flawed senses) and so they preclude our being able to act skilfully. With clear thinking, skilful action may lead to a solution of the problem and, if there is no solution, one is at least enabled to accept the present condition and go on to something better than pain, anger and refusing to accept any personal responsibility.

The mind that is free of clinging and craving is a mind free of worry. The mind free of worry is able to concentrate fully on the task in hand, be it a mental or a physical task. The mind free of worry is able to expand beyond petty, imaginary problems. Such a mind knows that it is not what happens to us that is of prime importance but how we react to it. If we are mentally busy clinging and craving, worrying about what we call security, our reactions will not be skilful and the outcome not what we had hoped for. The old saying 'count to ten before reacting' is good advice. For the religious Buddhist, saying a few mantras, especially the mantras of a favoured deity, has the same purpose.

Buddhism and Culture
Buddhism is many layered; it has almost as many layers as there are 'believers' and certainly as many layers as there are *cultural* beliefs onto which the basic teachings have been grafted. Much of what is written in this book would probably not be recognised by many who consider themselves Buddhists. The 'average' religious Buddhist is greatly concerned with craving for, and clinging to, wealth and good fortune in this life and a better time still in the next, and the next, and the next, *ad infinitum*, as are most of us. One life or many, our cravings remain the same.

The grafting of Buddhism onto those cultures that already practise deity worship (the worship of supernatural beings) has the advantage for the worshipper that there is a deity suitable to their psychological and emotional needs. If one believes in deities, then it is accepted that some are benign and helpful, and others wrathful and mischievous. The benign are venerated and receive devotion while wrathful ones need ritual placation. Ancestor worship appears to some Western eyes to resemble deity worship so closely as to be synonymous with it. Many Asian people believe strongly that their ancestors are still with them in spirit and very much capable of interfering in their lives for good or evil, depending on the character of the ancestor when they were alive. There are very beautiful ceremonies carried out in temples by monks and nuns with a family member or representative present to make the food and drink offerings to the deceased. These ceremonies carry on without a break from one generation to another. In this way family members are kept aware that all their actions are done under the watchful eyes of all who have gone before. If the family honour is blemished, the ancestors will see to it that the culprit, even the whole family, will be punished. This is their interpretation of Karma (or reward and punishment) at work.

Religious Buddhism
For the religious Buddhist, there are heavens and hells to be considered. These 'realms' differ according to the pre-Buddhist beliefs of a given culture. For example, in Tibetan Buddhist religious teachings there are three hot and three cold hells—all mental states—but often accepted as 'fact' by followers. There are said to be various heavenly realms (the abodes of the gods), wonderful, but impermanent. The hellish realms are as horrifying as the particular cultural imagination can make them, but they are also impermanent: no *everlasting* glory, no *everlasting* torment. Where are these heavens and hells? Let me relate an incident I witnessed some years ago at Chenrezig Institute at Eudlo in Queensland.

Geshè Nahwang Darghy was the visiting guru (teacher). Geshè-la is a quite famous teacher of Tibetan Buddhism, a man of great wisdom and compassion and an outstanding Mahayana scholar. He was teaching, from actual texts, an audience of monks, nuns, residents and visitors. When this is done in the West, the teacher reads what is written in the woodblock-printed text (original translations obtained from China and India when Buddhism was first introduced) and an interpreter is always used. Geshè had read the text on the heavenly realms and went on to the hellish realms. Most people are horrified by these texts (not listening when they are told that these are simply realms of the mind) though many, like children hearing a frightening fairy story, seem to relish them. Not so a middle-aged Dutch couple, who had spent every day of the seminar snorting cynically. They sat stiffly on chairs pushed as far back as the walls allowed.

Question time followed the reading, and as usual the questions showed various degrees of understanding. Geshè-la answered through his interpreter. The Dutch woman stood up and put her question *very* firmly: 'Would the Geshè kindly indicate to us the *exact geographical position* of these hell realms?'

Geshè-la chuckled softly as the interpreter told him the question. Then he replied, and this was the translation: 'Geshè-la says to ask you—where is your mind?' At this, the lady and her husband stood up and stamped out of the gompa (temple), slamming the doors behind them. They packed their campervan and left that day.

Those people had been handed a portion of wisdom which, if they had analysed it and meditated on it, would have been invaluable. Instead, they thought they had been insulted. Heaven and hell are certainly in our minds. We are in heaven or hell almost every day of our lives. Like rebirth, heaven and hell are experienced in this life. If they are experienced elsewhere, well, we will find out—or we won't.

If the belief in future heavens and hells is all that will

affect certain, almost impenetrable, mentalities, causing those with such mentalities to be more aware of the effects of their actions of body, speech and mind, then those teachings are considered worthwhile. In certain circumstances, such as when the listeners are illiterate, such beliefs may work better than human-made laws and prohibitions.

THE TEN FETTERS

Buddhism teaches that there are ten main fetters to our attempt to reach enlightenment, ten fetters that keep us on a roundabout of unskilful behaviour. These are:

1. Belief in an inherently, permanently existing 'self'.
2. Scepticism regarding these fetters.
3. Belief in 'purification' through rules and rites.
4. Sensual lust (for whatever we desire).
5. Ill-will.
6. Craving for rich material existence.
7. Craving for rich *immaterial* existence.
8. Conceit.
9. Restlessness.
10. Ignorance.

In Buddhist literature, be it doctrinal or popular, there are many such numbered lists, due to the ease with which they can be committed to memory. Lists are far easier to repeat than trying to remember prose word for word, and they are the way many people, even today, are able to repeat family lineages, history, legends and myths without the aid of writing.

Another list is called The Seven Jewels of the Awakened Ones:

1. Full trust in the Triple Refuge (Buddha, Dharma, Sangha).
2. Purity of morality.
3. Generosity.
4. Acquisition of right knowledge.
5. Industriousness.
6. Self-restraint in the light of social and environmental considerations.
7. Conscientious conduct.

Part of the early education of Buddhist monks and nuns has always been to learn, parrot fashion, tremendous amounts of texts. This method was necessary for the illiterate and was also the best means of preserving teachings without errors. In a group recital, or an individual recital before a group, mistakes are immediately obvious and will be corrected, whereas, in copying texts, mistakes do occur and are then repeated when the copy is copied, or written words may be translated incorrectly or interpreted incorrectly, according to the beliefs or mindset of the translator.

Some of these lists go back to basic Buddhism and some are the result of later philosophical thought on the Buddha's teachings from various points of view. It is of great interest to read several commentaries, each by a different 'authority', on the same text and note the different directions from which each scholar approaches the work and the conclusions offered. This can, of course, be confusing, but not if one is prepared to analyse and finally form one's own conclusions (without clinging to these as the *only* correct conclusions).

It may seem unnecessarily depressing for a religion to keep harping on the distressing side of life to people who are healthy, well fed, cherished and ambitious, and with excellent future prospects, or to those who are even half so fortunate. Yet these are often the ones least aware of impermanence and, therefore, the most devastated when circumstances alter for them. The people with less are well and truly aware that existence is no bed of thornless roses. Unfortunately, even this knowledge does not necessarily instil wisdom but often develops cravings beyond mere *wanting*.

UNIVERSAL COMPASSION

Human beings are not born equal except in their nakedness and in being subject to dukha, and in that we are all brothers and sisters. To become aware of these universal conditions should surely be the first step toward universal compassion.

Universal compassion does not mean having physical contact with ignorant (as in ignorant of skilful behaviour) or unpleasant people. It does not require the patting of hungry, unhappy wild animals or giving room to funnel-web or redback spiders in the house. It does not even require us to weep over an obnoxious neighbour and show them the 'error of their ways' to save them. Universal compassion means awareness at all times, and in regard to *all sentient beings*, that everything that lives experiences dukha. If it weren't for the Third Noble Truth we'd have to blame our suffering on some 'other', create a god or a demon and then go to a great deal of trouble to placate our creation.

The **Third Noble Truth** states simply that there *is* a way out of dukha. It is not to be won through rites, rituals and submission to superstitions. The way out of the effects of dukha is embarked upon at the very moment one becomes truly aware of the real condition of existence. This awareness may begin as a momentary spark and may just as suddenly be gone. But once experienced, it will happen again. It would be overwhelming, frustrating and the cause of severest depression if one could find no relief from suffering.

For religious Buddhists it is essential to find a way out of the continuing cycle of birth and death because Karma is forever nipping at their heels. For them to deliberately ignore the fact of dukha, once having become aware of it, would lead to heedless, manic behaviour and make for a horrible rebirth after this life. Religious Buddhists know that it would be no better if they had never become aware of the inevitability of dukha, because that would mean they must reincarnate again and again, preferably as human male beings (a pre-Buddhist belief), until they did become aware of dukha and, in becoming aware, have the opportunity to do something positive about it.

For the non-religious Buddhist it simply makes good sense to behave in such a way as to lessen the painful effects of dukha. Dukha cannot be ignored, but karma can be controlled by doing one's best to follow the Eightfold Path.

The steps of the Eightfold Path are not rules, regulations or commandments, but guidelines for beginning a life as free from suffering as one can personally make it. The main purpose of the Buddha's teaching was to help sentient beings—us—to live happier lives through *understanding*, not through obeying rules and regulations or bankrupting ourselves making offerings in the belief that help comes from 'out there' or 'up there'.

Sin

There is no concept of 'sin' in Buddhism that equates it with the Biblical concept. There is the awareness of ignorance of what is skilful or unskilful behaviour. Following the Eightfold Path and living by the Five Precepts is skilful behaviour. Doing harm to others or the environment and ignoring karma (cause and effect) is unskilful. There being no commandments to follow, the responsibility of one's choice of behaviour is entirely personal. One chooses, consciously or otherwise, the direction one's steps will take. As Buddha said, we go where our minds go. Let the mind dwell on snap judgments, flawed concepts and ill-considered, hard-held opinions and conflicts with others will soon arise, to be followed by unskilful reactions that call for more of the same on both sides. In this way, lifelong enmity and vendettas can and do arise.

Turning the Other Cheek

Buddhists, religious or non-religious, are not expected to be meek and mild goody-goodies, or punching-bags for the belligerent, standing silent when wrongfully accused. If they should remain calm and silent under such treatment it would only be because such behaviour seemed the most skilful under the circumstances. It is not a matter of 'peace at all costs', but a matter of wishing to cause no harm to *anyone*. There is a time to be firm, to appear almost wrathful if this seems the best way to act in given circumstances and with the type of persons with whom one is dealing.

The *motive* for one's choice of action is the important

point. One is not wrathful out of feelings of anger and hatred—emotions one has by now overcome—but out of compassion. The person confronting one is, perhaps, in need of firmness on our part, but compassionate firmness. Buddhists seek to do no harm to others, to the minds or the bodies.

Surely there should be no intolerance toward a religion that has never been involved in a religious war in all its long history, a religion that has always tolerated the beliefs of others, a religion that sees all living creatures as important to life on earth. There need be no fear of the Buddhist religion 'taking over' in Australia or anywhere else. Buddhism does not seek converts. It offers a treasure map for acceptance or rejection as we wish, with the suggestion that we take the directions to the treasure as directions only, rather than assume the map itself is the treasure. If the directions don't make sense to your mind, then that is OK too. *Que será, será.*

BUDDHA'S ADVICE FOR INDIVIDUALS

I would like to emphasise that in this book I am speaking on the mundane level of basic Buddhist teachings. To speak on any other level would require a quite different work. This work is written for the ordinary person who is trying to live as happily and comfortably as possible in the world in which we have to function. It is also written for those who are open-minded enough and mentally flexible enough to consider a different point of view, whether merely out of curiosity or in the hope of finding a way out of the dukha that is our common experience.

One of the teachings of the Buddha that could be of use

to all is the teaching he gave to the people of the kingdom of Kesaputta. These people were collectively known as Kalamas. They were puzzled and in doubt as to what to believe when every recluse, Brahmana (believers in Brahma, their supreme god) and ascetic insisted that *their* truth was *the* truth. This was Buddha's advice to them:

> Yes, Kalamas, it is proper that you have doubt, that you have perplexity, for a doubt has arisen in a matter which is doubtful. Now, look you Kalamas, do not be led by reports, or tradition, or hearsay. Be not led by the authority of religious texts, nor by mere logic or inference, nor by considering appearances, nor by the delight in speculative opinions, nor by seeming possibilities, nor by the idea: 'this is our teacher'. But, O Kalamas,when you know for yourselves that certain things are wholesome and good, then accept them and follow them.
>
> *Anguttara-nikaya sutra*

Buddha told the Sangha to examine even him, so that the disciples could be sure about the teacher they followed and thus have no doubt about the teaching—doubt being one of the five hindrances to enlightenment, if not used as an investigative tool.

Unfortunately, we humans are astonishingly adept at self-delusion. We usually don't even have to lie to ourselves in order to be quite sure that what we desire is 'good and wholesome'. Even some citizens of those nations practising genocide by using that obscene phrase 'ethnic cleansing' are able to believe that what they are doing is 'good and wholesome' and in the best interests of humanity.

Buddhism, philosophical or religious, can be of no real value to an individual unless one learns to be perfectly honest with oneself. Not to learn this leaves one simply 'going through the motions', conforming to one's cultural customs, trying to accept another culture, or even shaving one's head and wearing the robe of one's tradition, ethnic or chosen, in the belief that this, in itself, will activate enlightenment.

Being honest with oneself about oneself is not so easy as it sounds. There are times for some when shame or regret cause such mental anguish it would be easier to scratch an open wound with a wire brush than to investigate the cause, to accept one's part of the responsibility, and then *let it go*. Buddhist practices, if fully understood, are wonderful therapy for the troubled mind and that is part of what Buddha was 'getting at'.

What is it that prevents us from facing the truth of our past, or our motives—our plots and schemes? Why is it that, for some, self-analysis is almost impossible, not to be achieved even at the moment of death? Is it because self-analysis might shatter our idea of our *self*—the 'person' we see ourselves to be and hope to make others see also? This *idea* of 'self' is our most precious possession and to lose it is, in cases where there is only a precarious mental balance, more than the psyche can bear. Mental 'breakdown' can result. Therefore, it is not advisable to 'preach' such doctrine to those who are badly mentally or psychologically unbalanced.

Buddhist teaching is that there is no 'self' as we are accustomed to perceive it. No inherently existing, eternal person, personality, soul, spirit or whatever we wish to call it. The key word, often missed by the metaphysically and mystically inclined is *inherently*. Our idea of 'self' is of a solid, unconnected-with-anything-else entity, which is unchanging—a permanent 'I' residing within the mortal body.

A person says: 'I am Joe/Joan Smith.' We may ask: 'Who is Joe/Joan Smith?' The person will usually point to their chest: '*I* am Joe/Joan Smith.' Then we can begin to investigate with some seemingly absurd questions:

'Is that torso to which you point J. Smith?'

'No.'

'Is the hand with which you point J. Smith?'

'No.'

'Are the legs on which that torso rests J. Smith?'

'No.'

'Is the mouth that frames these replies J. Smith?'

We could carry on in this way until we had metaphorically shredded the flesh of J. Smith and drawn out the very marrow of the bones. A Zen Master might give the person before him an almighty whack with his staff and tell them to get out and come back when they had found J. Smith.

The simple answer, of course, is that 'J. Smith' is merely a label used for that particular, ever-changing, part-of-everything-else bundle of energy. This process of investigation can be carried out on any object we care to name. No *thing* can be said to inherently exist, only atomic particles that are continually changing form and position. This is what Buddhism calls emptiness—the void (modern scientific findings), taught by the Buddha more than 2,500 years ago. (A teacher is recommended, even necessary, for the understanding of this philosophy.)

Of what use to suffering individuals can this rather esoteric knowledge be? When phenomena are seen as unconnected and unchanging we may make hasty, mistaken judgments, for example, we may truly believe that the Blue Mountains are blue, as at a distance they appear to be. We believe that the person who did not reply to our greeting despises us. We turn discussions into arguments, even wars, because we see those whose ideas differ from ours as wicked enemies. We seem to be incapable of accepting people as they are without putting our own labels on them—just letting them be, giving them the respect and space we hope to receive ourselves. We see everything as good/bad, right/wrong, nice/nasty and so on.

We *all* experience dukha. This is a *general* condition, although we cannot know, without being shown, what particular experiences another is going through. We jump to conclusions based on what we think are 'facts', but they are really only our own *concepts* and *perceptions*, which we gather with limited faculties.

It is not necessary for everyone to agree with everyone else, except to agree to practise 'is it my business?'–style compassion. We need to see as clearly as possible what really *is*, in order to be able to act in the most skilful (useful) way, and, by our actions, do no harm.

In the world today we see how often good intentions lead to poor outcomes. With great desire to alleviate suffering we send material aid to those who need it. Sometimes that aid rots or is stolen and the only ones to benefit (temporarily) are those who will be enabled to cause more suffering.

Should our aid enable the former 'victims' to overcome their enemies, they may become the 'oppressors', and those we saw as the 'oppressors' may become the 'victims'. Thus, 'compassion' can not only be wasted but could lead to more, now vengeful, retaliation. Surely it is worthwhile to at least attempt to find a way out of this condition. But where to begin? That question is, for Buddhism, the easiest of all to answer. Thousands of years of political, social and religious attempts to overcome the ills of existence have failed. Oh, there have been some improvements but they can be wiped out by wars, famines and the natural disasters we have contributed to by short-sighted policies, greed, hatred and ignorance of how things really are.

The answer to this most important of questions is that, according to Buddhism, seeing more clearly how things really are must begin right where you are sitting. It begins with each one of us, each one of all the billions on earth, now and forever.

GREED, HATRED, IGNORANCE

Here is a good enough place for the individual to begin accepting that we all suffer, to a greater or lesser degree, from these conditions. This is one of the most basic Buddhist teachings and every practising Buddhist attempts, by whichever suggested method works best for them, to control their own greed, hatred and ignorance.

Greed
Greed, in this present case, refers to craving and clinging. It includes covetousness, envy and jealousy. It is the irrational craving for that which cannot possibly be obtained by the sufferer, either because of a lack of capability or a lack of ability to see an opportunity when it arises, or because the object of desire 'belongs' to someone else, or is in some way completely out of the sufferer's reach. Greed

is suffering, part of dukha. Greed, even if satisfied for a short time, leads to lack of lasting satisfaction; and over-indulgence, in turn, leads to revulsion. But we are slow to learn and immediately saturation is achieved we change the focus of our craving. 'Grand passions' usually end in tragedy. Tristan and Isolde, Aida, Othello and so on. Perhaps the real tragedy would be to see passionate desire deteriorate after thirty or forty years into petty inter-family feuds as it does so often in everyday life. Though some people's passionate love may last until death, clinging to 'what has been' is dukha, and dreadful loss and grief are often caused by our not anticipating change.

Greed can almost be said to be our natural condition, the natural condition of all that lives. We are born in a state of *desirousness*, for the sake of survival. Without the desire for food we would die. At first, greed is instinctive and necessary, but as the intellect develops, sheer greed does not always decrease but remains as strong as ever. In this permanent state of desirousness, our attention is captured by something—we are attracted to 'it', to 'him' or to 'her', and at that moment our 'desire' is transferred to it or them. The object may be animate (a person or animal) or inanimate (jewels, buildings, landscapes, whatever). Then the problem of desire is compounded by the expectation that the desired object will never change in any way from our flawed concept of its 'reality'.

No matter what is gained in life—comfort, love, wealth, fame—we are never satisfied. With all 'desires' gained we still want more or something else. There is dukha—lack of lasting satisfaction—in every life, no matter how fortunate, unless we become aware of imper-manence. Buddhist practices are for the achievement of that awareness.

The Buddhist antidote to greed is generosity—generosity in material giving with clear insight as to its usefulness to the recipient, and in developing a generosity of spirit, the sincere wish to give to all sentient beings whatever it is they need for comfort and happiness. It's a readiness to give help where needed, not to be a rabid do-gooder, rushing into others' affairs, sure that we have the only solution to a situation we may not fully understand. Without clear-sightedness, even trying to develop an antidote can cause further suffering.

Greed and craving go with clinging and are part of it. Clinging is part of greed. Greed says, 'What is mine is mine and what is yours is mine', while clinging adds, 'And I am not going to give it back and I want more of it'. The more we cling to 'things' (ideas, opinions, material possessions, even mistaken memories and certainly emotional relationships), the greater the distress when change becomes apparent. To lose what is 'possessed', or to have our prized opinions and concepts proven wrong, is painful in proportion to the strength with which we cling to them. This clinging is what Buddhists call 'attachment'.

Hatred
Hatred is another source of suffering, for it destroys the hater's mind. Hatred is excessive aversion. There is a Buddhist practice that helps overcome hatred. We are required, first of all, to explore deeply the reasons for our hatred. Sometimes we hate that in another person which we see, or are afraid of developing, in ourselves. Sometimes we hate simply because we do not understand or are mistaken about the object of our aversion. Sometimes we hate because our beliefs are challenged and we know we are unable to uphold them. We allow ourselves to be

humiliated and then, with hatred, seek revenge. All this has searing effects on character, but those effects can be overcome.

One method for overcoming hatred is based on the mental practice of exchanging self for others. It is based on the belief in reincarnation and states that if we have lived countless lives and will reincarnate countless more times, then we have all had a different status and even a different sex. The enemy of today has been, at some time, one's loving mother or father, sister or brother, husband or wife, child or lover. The beloved of today may once have been an enemy, and a person to whom one is completely indifferent has been any or all of the above.

The practice involves quiet meditation: imagining a loved one to one's right, the hated one to the left, and the neutral one in front. Then one begins to mentally exchange one for the other, and for one's self, until the futility of clinging to one's hatred becomes apparent. When next confronted with the object of hatred, one recognises the insubstantiality of the hatred, the loving kindnesses you have shared in past lives, and excessive aversion subsides. If the hatred began because of an injury done to us, it is overcome by compassion for the injurer, whom we now see as a fellow-sharer in dukha.

As stated above, hatred is *excessive* aversion. Before we attain enlightenment, a certain amount of natural aversion is often useful for keeping us from indulging in unwholesome behaviour. Enlightenment is beyond aversion and non-aversion.

Ignorance

Ignorance, as the word is used in Buddhism, is ignorance of the Dharma, ignorance of the way things really are at

this moment, ignorance of right knowledge. This ignorance is the cause of our unfortunate mistakes. Ignorance
is simply *not knowing*. It is not a slur on one's intelligence
or education—simply the state of being unaware of the
illusory nature of existence. It is as though we had arrived
in a country where we were completely ignorant of the
laws, the language, the very terrain. So our best intentions, in that case, could still have the most unfortunate
consequences.

Buddhism stresses the importance of volition or
motive. We need to be constantly aware of our motives
for a certain course of action. If the motive is right, so,
usually, is the outcome. Here one must be aware of the
situation where a disastrous outcome is excused on the
grounds that one 'meant well'. 'Meant well' seldom does
well. If one is generous with the hope of reward, or kind
with the hope of an enhanced reputation, then motive is
questionable. Giving needs to be giving for its own sake,
and kindness needs to be given with no attachment to
receiving thanks or recognition as a benefactor.

Body, Speech and Mind
Buddhism also stresses awareness of the actions of one's
own body, speech and mind. We speak nowadays of
'body language' and like to think we can read this 'language' in others, but we do not pay enough attention to
the actions of our own body. We can use our body to do
great harm or we can use it skilfully. Speech is the most
direct form of communication and, here again, we can
use it for harm, to slander, to insult, to insinuate or to
humiliate, or we can speak only kindly, truthfully and not
indulge in gossip. The mind 'drives' the body. Buddha
reminded his followers that where the mind goes *with*

attachment, the body goes. Mental lust leads to physical action, be it desire to possess the body of a person or the property of another. Cruel thoughts are forerunners of cruel actions, erroneous thoughts lead to erroneous, unskilful reactions to circumstances. The person aware of body, speech and mind will practise to keep the mind in wholesome channels, eschewing unkind, lascivious or destructive thoughts.

Anger

Anger is better eliminated than controlled. Anger is like pressure, and controlled pressure requires a safety valve. Often the safety valve used is violence (verbal or physical), which may become the cause of as much trouble as the original anger would have been. The way to eliminate anger is to use analytical meditation. After preparation, one brings the anger to mind and then, without emotion, investigates the *real* cause of it. In most cases it happens that the cause is a bruised ego. Somehow the person with whom one is angry has attacked one of our most precious opinions or a much-prized self-concept. A less 'self'-centred cause of anger is often indignation at injustice to oneself or others. The indignation is excellent fuel for skilful action, but anger only clouds judgment and triggers unskilful, unhelpful reactions.

FOR WHOM DID BUDDHA TEACH?

Buddhism is not only for those capable of heroic ascetic practices, holy hermits, scholars and philosophers, and monks and nuns. Monasteries were only an outcome of Buddhism, not the intended outcome of the Buddha's wish to impart the Dharma. Buddha spoke to ordinary laypeople, some of whom later became monks and nuns because that was their need, but the Dharma was for all. It was not expected that anyone should change their way of life unless their way of life was causing, or was capable of causing, harm to others, for example, murdering, thieving, or working in armaments or with poisons.

When asked for advice by kings and rulers, Buddha told them to rule with justice, to see to the wellbeing of their subjects. He pointed out that poverty was a cause of robbery, so workers should be paid just wages. Attention should be paid to seeing that storehouses were kept stocked against times of need such as drought, floods and other natural disasters. He gave advice about the likely outcome of armed conflict with neighbouring states.

Business people also sought the Buddha's advice. To these, he said to treat their workers and servants with kindness and fairness in all matters. His advice to workers and servants was to be honest and diligent in their work. He also advised business people to divide their income into four, and to use one part for business purposes, one for their own needs and the maintenance of their family, one part for charitable concerns and to put the fourth part aside for future needs.

SOCIAL BEHAVIOUR

There are six main courses of social behaviour advised by the Buddha for the individual.

1. **Parents are sacred to their children** In good Buddhist families, children 'worship' their parents every

day by performing duties in the way of love, respect and physical assistance. Parents should keep their children from unsuitable situations (bad company etc.); should provide them with good activities; should give them a good education; should marry them into good families; and should hand over the family property to them in due course.

2. **The relation between teacher and pupil** provides that pupils should respect and be obedient to teachers; should attend to their needs if any; and should study earnestly. The teacher should train and shape the pupil properly; should introduce the pupil to friends; and should try to procure the pupil security or employment when the pupil's education is completed.

3. **The relationship of husband and wife** holds that love between spouses is considered sacred, almost religious. Husband and wife should be faithful, respectful and devoted to each other; the husband should secure the wife's comfort and position, and please her with gifts of clothing and jewellery (this alone should show the Buddha's esteem for women). The wife should supervise and look after household affairs; should entertain guests, visitors, friends, relatives and employees; should protect family earnings; and should be energetic and clever in all activities.

4. **The relations between friends, relatives and neighbours** should be hospitable. They should be charitable to one another; should speak pleasantly and agreeably; should work for one another's welfare; should be on equal terms with one another; should not quarrel amongst themselves; should help one another in need; and should not forsake one another in difficulty.

5. **The relation between employer and employee**
   The employer has several obligations toward his
   employees: work should be assigned according to
   capacity and ability; medical needs should be provided
   and occasional bonuses granted. Employees should be
   diligent, obedient and not cheat their employer; they
   should be earnest in their work.
6. **The relations between Brahmins, recluses and
   laypeople** The laypeople should look after the material needs of the religious with love and respect; the
   religious with a loving heart should impart knowledge
   and learning to the laity and lead them on the good
   path away from evil doing. (The 'clergy' were the
   teachers in India.)

RITES, RITUALS AND CEREMONIES

The Buddhist has no need to attend external rites and
rituals but there are, in every country, ceremonies on
religious occasions. Followers of Mahayana, Vajrayana
and other Mahayana sects do have many rituals and rites,
some exotic, all benign, with very special significance for
the participants.

There is nothing pertaining to the Buddhist religion
that should arouse disquiet in the minds or emotions of
other religious observers. There is no custom of converting people to Buddhism. Quite the contrary, no Buddhist
will *tell* you anything unless you ask. The present writer
would not have put pen to paper without being asked to
do so. But once the questions are asked, there is a wealth
of information to be had on whatever level the questioner
happens to require it.

HIDDEN SECRETS

There is, in certain Mahayana works, talk of 'secret' or 'hidden' knowledge. This means only that until these matters have been explained to the initiate they remain unknown or 'secret'. In the same way we would find technical texts difficult to understand without explanation. They would be 'secret' as far as we are concerned. Another example might be the internal combustion engine or how a computer works—all 'secret' until explained to us. Much adult knowledge is 'secret' from children through lack of experience and ability to understand. Such things need explanation when we are ready and able to understand. Until that time, the knowledge is 'secret' or hidden from us. No-one will prevent us from learning the 'secrets' if we really wish to know. That is what teachers are for.

Some 'secret' information is not written, even in this day and age, but is transmitted orally from teacher to disciple, who in turn passes it on to other disciples. In this way, the information is secret where non-disciples are concerned, but it is not a personal secret. This statement means that whatever a Buddhist teacher passes on to disciples is not a personal opinion but the teachings of the particular Buddhist sect to which the teacher belongs. There are no 'secrets', nothing is 'hidden' from those seeking information.

The *Dhammapada* consists of more than 400 very short statements, most quite easily understood by Buddhists and non-Buddhists without explanation, with this exception: it is wise to obtain the most up-to-date translation from the original that one can find. Verse 50 is excellent advice for anyone wishing to 'make a new start'. The first translators were Theosophists, not Buddhists, and they translated according to their personal understanding.

> One should not pry into the faults of others,
> into things done and left undone by *others*. [my italics]
> One should rather consider what by oneself is
> done and left undone. (Verse 50)

Or this:

> Hatred is never appeased by hatred in this world;
> it is appeased by love.
> This is an eternal law. (Verse 5)

K. Dharmaratana Thera (ed.), Dhammapada

Buddhism is not so lofty, so sublime, as to be beyond the power of ordinary people to understand and practise. The teachings are *for* ordinary people; the teachings may even help them to become *extraordinary* people. Buddhism is not an esoteric doctrine requiring one to retire to a cave or to the desert or a monastery. Such isolation would be of one's own choosing and for one's own reasons. (I'll discuss this later in the section on monasticism.)

Buddha taught what he taught for the comfort and happiness of all types of people. Monks and nuns are not necessarily the *best* Buddhists. The *best* Buddhists—monks, nuns or laypeople—are the ones who strive to understand correctly what *really is*; the ones who strive to analyse their own concepts, their own view of existence, the reasons why they react as they do; the ones who strive to be constantly aware (mindful) of what is happening around and within themselves; the ones for whom doing no harm has become effortlessly their way of living.

Buddhists are not expected to emulate a god or a super-natural being. The goal of enlightenment is achievable by any earnest person in this very lifetime. Believing there will be many human lifetimes in which to achieve enlightenment makes a fine excuse for not trying now.

ULTIMATE AND CONVENTIONAL TRUTH

There are for Buddhists (and for physicists) two forms of truth. In Buddhism these are called conventional truth and ultimate truth. For many Western minds, such an assertion causes great difficulty in that we are accustomed to the idea that truth is truth is truth. We are not all trained physicists.

The explanation of these two truths is really quite simple and can be expressed in several ways on a mundane level, keeping in mind that these are important matters and full understanding requires analysis, concentration and meditation.

The Buddhist theory of emptiness—lack of inherent existence of all compound phenomena, or dependent origination, rather similar to the theory of relativity—is, as stated earlier, existence as it is now being explained by physics. When one examines any 'thing' minutely, right down to its photons, neutrons and beyond, one finds a vast 'emptiness'. The 'thing' examined does not exist as we are accustomed to perceive it. This, in Buddhist philosophy, is very simply put: the ultimate truth is that all is illusion, impermanence.

The second truth, or conventional truth, is the truth with which we function in the world, accepting the five sense-based perceptions as reality. Physicists who have seen 'ultimate truth' through experiments and theories still drive to a 'real' home in a 'real' car after daily work and find no difficulty in doing so. They use 'real' instruments of investigation, write 'real' reports at a 'real' desk—all of which they *know* to be 'unreal', yet they are able to make use of these 'things' that exist *conventionally*. A Buddhist aims to be as constantly 'mindful' as possible of the two types of truth.

It may seem to some that full awareness, realisation of ultimate truth, would make normal life impossible; it would cause all sorts of physical and mental difficulties. A little consideration will show that, on the contrary, it can help us to see situations or events more clearly and to react more skilfully, avoiding unpleasant or even dangerous retaliations or reactions.

Not all who are known as Buddhist have the inclination or even the capability to *investigate* the philosophy on which their religion is built. Therefore they tend to be eclectic, choosing (consciously or not) those given teachings most acceptable to themselves. So they offer prayers, carry out strict rituals, believe the historical stories and folktales which suit them best or which they feel they should believe, and in this way they absorb into their lives whatever helps them to live the way they choose. There is no fault to be found in this, the usual way of existence for most of us, although there is the danger of accepting whatever one is told without vigorously investigating it for oneself as the Buddha advised. We humans are a mentally lethargic lot in many ways.

Who Wants Nirvana?
Not all Buddhists are actively seeking to become fully enlightened. Buddhist religion and faith in what they are

told is enough for many. Not all Buddhists have read any of the sutras, or studied the philosophical treatises of those who followed the Buddhist way and wrote over the centuries. Many ethnic Buddhists cannot read, and some have no Dharma translations in their own language. Others, even with translations available, are not of an investigative turn of mind. For these people, faith is enough to help them live decent lives, doing no harm to themselves or to others, and that alone is a great achievement for anyone.

At the other end of the scale, there are the metaphysical philosophers, those whose deep investigative thinking may or may not show them the way to enlightenment, but whose works can be stepping stones for many, provided nothing is taken on trust. It cannot be repeated too often: Buddhism is a matter of personal experience.

In the *Sabba Sutta Samyutta Nikaya*, the Buddha states:

> Monks [meaning in this sutra monks, nuns and disciples—in short, sangha; not simply Sangha or monastic members] I will teach you 'everything'. Listen to it. What, monks, is 'everything'? Eye and material form, ear and sound, nose and odour, tongue and taste, body and tangible objects, mind and mental objects. These are called 'everything'. Monks, he who would say: 'I will reject this everything and proclaim another everything', he may certainly have a theory (of his own). But when questioned, he would not be able to answer and would, moreover, be subject to vexation. Why? Because it would not be within the range of experience (avisaya).

This quotation shows the 'down-to-earth' nature of the Buddha's teaching. He was not offering a 'future life' solution to the human condition. Always he guided his hearers toward a feet-on-the-ground, 'you can do it' solution based on human ability rather than on some 'grace' arbitrarily given by a supernatural source. The Buddha didn't deal in airy-fairy theories but in human experience in the here and now, based on individual capability.

While the above quotation may appear to make the great 2,539-year-old teaching seem mundane, cut-and-dried theories, it should be remembered that all the words ever written on Buddhism, all the speeches made, esoteric initiations conferred, even highest ordinations, will not clearly express what is ultimately a personal experience. All the craving of a lifetime for enlightenment is only adding one more craving, it is one more desire to add to our basic 'desirousness'. Our own personal experience is the way—the way to see clearly and to use that clear-sightedness to negate our difficulties, so many of which we construct ourselves from ignorance of what *is* at this moment.

Buddha proclaimed insight into the true nature of phenomena as the sole means to emancipation. The entire body of Buddhist philosophical and religious teaching consists of nothing more than signposts or treasure maps, which we continue to mistake for the goal or the treasure.

3

BUDDHISM IN DIFFERENT CULTURES

Theravada, Mahayana and Zen

৵

A WESTERN BHIKKHUNI

Incense was firmly moulded with wax into small cones, three of which were placed in line across the freshly shaven scalp of each of the six women sitting cross-legged on the floor. A burning taper was then applied to each cone in turn. As the cones smouldered, silent tears slid from under the lowered eyelids of one of the women, while some of the others pressed their lips firmly

together. The onlookers almost held their breath watching for signs of weakness, or perhaps even hoping for
them. On one head, a cone crumbled and fell in tiny
burning fragments on to the grey garments of the woman.
She made no move. A fresh cone was moulded, reapplied
to her head, and lit. As the woman involved in this
mishap was the oldest in the group, she was carefully
and compassionately observed by those controlling the
ordeal.

After some fifteen or twenty minutes, the cones were
consumed and antiseptic dressings applied to the
women's smarting scalps. The women then rose and
bowed deeply towards the officiants and to those who
had quietly encouraged them. The sufferers now donned
yellow robes over their grey ones, and the number of
'patches' making up each yellow robe indicated that these
women were bhikkhunis.

What had been going on here? Who were these
women? Who were these controllers? Who was being
tested? By whom? And to what purpose?

The women dressed in grey only were laywomen,
Vietnamese; the ones undergoing the 'burning' were
ordained Buddhist nuns. The nationalities of the six nuns,
who had the previous day received highest ordination,
were: Australian, Dutch, French, Spanish and Vietnamese
(two women). I was the one on whose scalp the cone
had crumbled.

The ceremony in which we had just taken part was
undertaken voluntarily from both a respect for custom
and personal conviction. It was also the latter part of a
three-day ritual, and the public part of the ordination
ceremonies—this part being the taking of bhodisattva
vows, a solemn Mahayana Buddhist initiation, here done

according to the Asian tradition. The initiates vowed to direct all their efforts toward helping every sentient being to eventual enlightenment. Now, by silently enduring the burning, we were, to use a colloquial term, 'putting our money where the mouth is', and proving our commitment to suffering whatever might be necessary to fulfil our vows.

Does it hurt? It certainly does. As to who is testing whom, the answer is that we were each testing ourselves because of some inner need to do so. The 'controllers' were the senior monks and nuns involved in the ordination ceremonies the previous day. It was all done in a spirit of love and support, with no pressure applied by anyone at any point.

Not all present-day sects of Buddhist religion practise this ritual. Today, nearly five years after full ordination (I was a novice for twelve years), my hair is long and worn in a bun, and my scars are likely to be noticed only by a hairdresser if I should ever avail myself of such services, or when I am residing in a monastery. They are of no interest to anyone but myself. Some monks and nuns go through this burning ceremony more than once, adding new scars to old. Why they do this only they know for sure. I can but speak for myself; I made a commitment that needs no reviving. I do not need further reminders of the vows I took in a Vietnamese temple, near Limoges in France, before the Patriarch, the Very Reverend Dr Thich Huyen-Vi, and the necessary witnesses.

As I write, what is commonly known as the Buddhist religion has risen to third place of religions professed or practised in Australia. In the event of continued Asian immigration to this country, that figure will rise. Even without further immigration it will rise due to Australian-born progeny of immigrants accepting, from choice or convention, the religion of their parents. We can either ignore this new—to us—set of beliefs or have enough interest to try to understand it.

THE BUDDHA'S NEW CLOTHES

The religious side of Buddhism grew out of a moral–social–psychological philosophy derived from the need of ordinary people within the religion's orbit to under-stand what was being taught. There was then—and is now—a most natural reluctance on the part of monks and teachers to give up old beliefs, to possibly throw the baby out with the bathwater. The innate tolerance of basic Buddhist teachings (regarding the needs and beliefs of all varieties of human mental capabilities and cultures) has caused the philosophy to become layered over the centuries with earlier beliefs. In other words, the Buddha has become swathed in many-coloured folds of needs and rich devotions, veiled so heavily that the original figure has sometimes become obscured.

Due to this manner of the spread of Buddha Sakya-muni's (the Sage of the Sakya clan) teachings there now exists an array of what we call Buddhist traditions. Some have little to do with what are now ascertained to be the original teachings, which were solely an effort to under-stand the fundamental principles of existence.

So, contemporary Buddhism is many-layered, and in order to make it intelligible to the non-Buddhist, or even to the pseudo-Buddhist, lay or monastic, or whoever is a 'by rote' Buddhist (as it were), there is a need to range rather far and wide. Hence the apparent ambition of this work on a subject at once so simple and so vast.

Any description of religious Buddhism will confuse the investigator in much the same way as a Protestant Christian may be perplexed by aspects of Roman or Orthodox Catholic doctrines or indeed by the contents of a church or cathedral of those religions. Yet something of the tolerance that is part of Buddhism has been applied by Catholicism to take in aspects of the beliefs and venerations important to other peoples and reinterpret and incorporate them into its rites and rituals. It would now be very difficult to present a picture of 'pure, uncontaminated' non-cultural Buddhism.

Very broadly speaking, there are today three main divisions of religious Buddhism, each of which is represented in Australia and indeed in the West. These are Mahayana, Theravada and Zen Buddhism. Each of these is divided further into sects which adhere to different interpretations of Buddhism by past and present teachers. These divisions have arisen over 2,500 years and some are of long standing while others are relatively recent.

THERAVADA

Theravada is generally known as the Southern appreciation of the teachings, reaching what was then called Ceylon from the reign of the Indian King Asoka in the third century BC. The learned Buddhist Mogaliputta-tissa was urged by Asoka to devise ways and means of refuting heretical ideas which by then had penetrated different Buddhist schools of philosophy, due to the influx of great numbers of people to influential and prosperous university–monasteries. Many newcomers were Brahmin, were not true followers of the Buddha's philosophies, and were often more interested in gaining their own advantage within what had become the state religion. The scriptural texts of the Southern School—its followers called Theravadins—were recorded in the Pali language, in contrast to Northern School texts which were recorded in Sanskrit. The first translations of Buddhist texts to reach the West were from the Pali.

MAHAYANA

Mahayana is today the most widespread of the 'sects' of Buddhist religion, appearing in China, Mongolia, Tibet, Vietnam, Japan and now in Australia. The main appeal of Mahayana lies in the belief in the bodhisattva ideal. The bodhisattva is what Christians and possibly Muslims would call a saint—one who stands at the gates of paradise through a life purely lived and who forgoes entry through those gates until every last being in the universe has passed through with the saint's help. In this context, Buddha Sakyamuni himself becomes a bodhisattva along with many others, yet he remains the great, supreme bodhisattva.

ZEN

Zen, which spread from India to China, then to Japan and now to the USA and Australia, is basically considered to be a very 'direct' path to enlightenment. It is also considered part of the Mahayana tradition. There is an *apparent* simplicity in Zen that appeals to the love of order and discipline in certain types of person. It is often thought of as the method of 'sudden' illumination. This is incorrect. Sudden illumination can be attained only after acquiring much wisdom and knowledge. If one has no idea what one is aiming for, there can be no recognition of whatever it is one finally attains. Really, sudden illumination is qualitative change after quantitative practice. Satori is similar to the bliss experienced upon the sudden resolution of a problem after we have worried ourselves sick over it and then flung the bothersome thing away. Suddenly—hey presto—there is the answer! Satori, the release of mental tension, is not permanent but a taste of the equanimity to come with true enlightenment.

A CHINESE OR VIETNAMESE CHUA

As most Australian Mahayana Buddhists are Chinese and Vietnamese, let us take a look into a Mahayana temple or chua. We will first have removed our shoes, as we would also do in a Theravada or Zen temple, or a Muslim mosque. Usually there will be floor covering, either matting of some kind, or carpeting. We are now inside the equivalent of a church and should, if from nothing more than good manners, behave as we would in any sacred place.

The main feature will probably be a triple altar with almost identical figures of a seated 'Buddha' with oriental features. The only differences will be in the position of the hands, each position having symbolic meaning. These figures are not meant to represent the actual features of Buddha Sakyamuni. They are symbols of serenity and non-attachment (not *un*attachment) and are meant to direct the mind of the observer to Buddhist values and moral principles as well as to the life of Buddha Sakyamuni. These statues are not meant to be aesthetically pleasing to Western perceptions and usually are not so, unlike the statues in a Catholic church, which tend to be of real, although idealised, human beings.

On a lower level, at the side altars, there will be elaborate statues of historical and legendary heroes who have become protectors and bodhisattvas. Behind these altars may be several other, smaller altars, some being used in death-rite ceremonies, which are paid for by families and carried out at certain specified intervals. There may also be an altar, very much revered, for the founder of the particular 'sect' or group owning the temple. Buddhism is not quite the strictly organised religion it may appear to be, there being no universal 'head' similar to the Roman Catholic Pope or the Anglican Archbishop of Canterbury. Each group of followers of any particular leader has complete autonomy. The 'leader' is usually a master (female or male) renowned for their teaching and supported by their followers. While there may be Patriarchs of different countries (masters acceptable to followers in a certain area or monastics of a given sect), there is no 'Patriarch of Patriarchs' as it were.

Back in the temple, the visitor will see a profusion of beautiful flowers, burning candles and incense, and well-arranged offerings of fruit and often money. These offerings are traditional in any branch of Buddhist religion. No food offerings of any type go to waste but are shared within the community, with monks and nuns, or wherever needed. As they have been given to the Buddha, one simply asks his permission to partake.

There will be ritual implements: gongs, drums, bells, hollow wooden fish, large and small beaten-metal cauldrons, candelabra and often a particular statue, haloed and many-armed, which represents the all-giving bodhisattva of mercy—Chenrezig to Tibetans and Quan Yin to others. Nowadays, to the utter horror of aesthetically minded Westerners, the statues may have haloes of bright neon tubing in what seems to us garish, clashing colours, which may be completely off-putting. Not so to the dedicated Buddhist, to whom the aesthetic value is quite irrelevant. Colours have symbolic meaning, differing slightly in different cultures, and may or may not complement each other in the eye of the beholder.

In Chinese and Vietnamese traditions, rituals are carried out before the altar, with celebrants and participants standing or kneeling. Chanting is done in a type of Chinese language that might be described as similar to Latin as it stands to Italian, or Sanskrit as it stands to its modern Indian derivatives. It is archaic, but the *meaning* of the prayers and chanted scriptures is understood through repetition. The language is traditional and ritualistic. Almost everyone uses the prayer books provided, just as the Catholic priest and congregation did during the Latin Mass prior to 1968. Those with excellent memories need no books.

Depending on the availability of monks and nuns, rituals are held at least three or four times daily. If monks are available they will lead; in their absence, a fully ordained nun (bhikkhuni) will lead and the novices assist her.

There is a solemn and impressive form of walking meditation with accompanying chanting during certain rituals inside the temple as well as elsewhere. A special

yellow robe is worn over the grey or brown or yellow
worn for all rituals, the number of patches in the yellow
robe indicating the seniority (in ordination, not age) of
the wearer. The words bhikkhu and bhikkhuni mean
fully ordained monk or nun, while the term master is
reserved for one well studied in Buddhism, fully ordained
for at least ten years and accepted as a master by his or
her disciples and followers.

Apart from the chanting, which is most pleasant, the
noise of bells, gongs and drums (even kettle drums) may
be distracting to the Western ear, but it is not random
noise and has ritual purposes.

Outside many Chinese and Vietnamese chuas will be
a large white statue of Quan Yin (whose mantra is
Quante Ambo Tat), the bodhisattva of mercy. Quan Yin
is a graceful, asexual figure, looking down compassionately from a many-petalled lotus pedestal. One circumam-
bulates, right shoulder to the statue, chanting 'Namo
Quante Ambo Tat', a prayer for compassion and mercy,
and telling the mantra on one's 108-bead 'rosary'. This is
marvellously soothing if things have lately been a bit out
of kilter.

A TIBETAN GOMPA

Tibetan Buddhism also has a devoted following in
Australia. The original centre and gompa (temple) were
established in the hills behind Eudlo in Queensland by a
group of 'seekers' who came under the influence of a
marvellously charismatic, wise and humble lama (monk)
whom they found in Nepal. This was Lama Thubten
Yeshè, now deceased. His disciple, Lama Thubten Zopa

Rinpoche (Tibetan for precious one—a reincarnation), while from a different 'sect' to Lama Yeshè, is now spiritual director. Let us now visit Chenrezig Institute for Wisdom Culture in its 64-hectare setting of bushland and tropical gardens.

Chenrezig Centre, as it is known to its residents and regular visitors, has a permanent resident geshè (a very senior monk), whose Tibetan Buddhist education can be likened to a doctorate in divinity. He has a translator who may be a Tibetan monk or a Western monk proficient in the Tibetan language and trained in Buddhist doctrine, or even a Tibetan layperson not necessarily religiously inclined. There is a small permanent community of nuns on the property. A group of lay Buddhists administer the centre, which holds special teaching programs and open days. These administrators are residents and there is visitor accommodation. Recently Chenrezig (named for the compassionate aspect of the Buddha nature) Centre celebrated its twentieth birthday.

The Dalai Lama, His Holiness Tenzin Gyatso, is considered by his people to be the reincarnation of Chenrezig in its bodhisattva form and as such is venerated by all 'sects' of Tibetan Mahayana Buddhism. The reincarnation is always considered to be Chenrezig as well as to be the reborn Dalai Lama and so, for a great many Tibetans and Tibetan Buddhists, the reigning Dalai Lama is always an incarnate Buddha. The present incarnation is known worldwide for his continuing work for peace. He is, as he often points out, only a simple Buddhist monk—an understatement if ever there was one.

Climbing the hill at Chenrezig Centre we pass first one, then another, prayer wheel. These are, in fact, large cylinders. They are filled with relics and strips of paper printed with the mantra, 'Om Mani Padme Hung', very loosely translated as, 'Hail to the jewel in the lotus', the jewel being Buddha Sakyamuni and holy relics. We spin the prayer wheel, which rings a bell calling the attention of the spirits to the offering of praise and prayer, then we climb the steps to the gompa.

Chenrezig Institute's gompa was my first experience of such a building and my first contact with Tibetan culture. I fancy I must have been expecting the visual serenity of an ancient, unpainted Grecian temple, with unadorned white marble statues and nothing even remotely resembling clutter and over-the-top ornamentation. I quite forgot that ancient Greek statues and buildings had been painted originally with awful, gaudy combinations of colour and only time has stripped them to purity.

Having been brought up a Catholic and having then sought a 'purer' spiritual experience, my first thought in the gompa was: 'Oh, no! I might just as well have stayed a Catholic!' I was sure I'd never find what I needed in that place—but find it I did, or at least I found the place on which to put my foot for that first step that begins any journey to anywhere—or nowhere.

There is an outer doorway to the gompa and an inner door, and before entering we remove our shoes. Once inside, we face the main altar with its brass Buddha image—one only. It may be helpful to repeat here that none of the statues in any branch of Buddhism is meant to be a physical likeness of the Buddha. They are all symbolic: symbols of repose, of wisdom, of non-attachment and of universal compassion. No real Buddhist worships a Buddha statue. They are not idols. The reverence, devotion and respect are for the memory of the teacher and his dharma (teachings).

Inside the gompa we may see people prostrating themselves three times before entering futher. They join their palms on top of their heads, then at the throat and the heart, and then fall to their knees, touching their forehead to the floor before proceeding to their cushion. Yes, cushion. In the Tibetan tradition one sits cross-legged, in the lotus position if possible, on a cushion. The height of the meditation cushion makes it easier to keep the spine straight. If this position is quite painful for certain people, Chenrezig Institute provides a few chairs. There is good reason for this seating position, which we will come to a bit later.

Most rituals are performed early in the morning, in the evening or at night. Depending on the date and phase of the moon, there may be several rituals. At other times there will be teachings from texts and commentaries on philosophical works given by the geshè, a monk or nun, or an advanced lay student.

Ordination in the Tibetan Tradition

The ordination of monks and nuns in the Tibetan tradition differs from the Chinese/Vietnamese/Japanese traditions for historical cultural reasons. Tibetan-ordained monks must undergo highest ordination in a Chinese/ Vietnamese tradition if they wish to act in that tradition, and Tibetan nuns are considered novices only (by non-Tibetans) until they take further bhikkhuni ordination if they wish. Most do not, being happy within what has become their own tradition. His Holiness the Dalai Lama hopes full ordination for women may be given to Tibetan nuns in the future, when enough novices have become bhikkunis with the necessary authority to ordain others.

In the gompa, there seems to the non-Buddhist to be

much unintelligible chanting (still mostly in the Tibetan language, for good reasons) and a great deal of strange 'music' at times. Again, a special yellow robe is always worn over Tibetan yellow and maroon robes for rituals and teachings being given directly from texts. Seniority is not by ordination, but by years since acceptance of the robes and vows, so the patches are identical in number for all nuns, unless they are also bhikkhunis, and for novice monks. The fully ordained have more patches.

A high 'throne' is placed before the main altar for the geshè when he is teaching or reading from texts; he may sit in a lower seat for general talks or lessons. The throne is not for the 'glory' of the reader but respect for the Buddha's teachings of the dharma.

To either side of the main altar are small altars holding statuettes of deceased lamas, dalai lamas and miniature stupas. Stupas are cairns or more elaborate structures holding holy relics, which may be cremated ashes or objects used by the saint or sage for whom the monument is raised. There will also be incense and written mantras. Stupa building is, for Mahayanists, considered to be an immense source of 'merit'.

At Chenrezig Institute, to the left as one faces the altar, is a life-sized plaster statue of an asexual human figure with many faces and a thousand outstretched arms positioned like the spokes of a wheel. In the palm of each hand is an eye and six of the hands hold ritual objects. Two hands hold between them at the heart level a jewel, the same wish-fulfilling jewel one offers in the palm-to-palm greeting—the namastè—with thumbs tucked in to represent the jewel. This figure is the bodhisattva Chenrezig, the Tibetan version of Quan Yin. The extra hands and faces symbolise the ability to see in all directions, so

Chenrezig is able to help thousands at one moment. The eyes in the hands represent clear-sightedness, so that no harm can result from would-be good deeds. This is, of course, only a brief explanation—to be noted by all would-be do-gooders who leap in with their own unconsidered ideas about what is best for others.

To the left as one faces the altar is another life-sized statue of a beautiful young woman, coloured green. She begins naked, dressed only in jewels and scanty draperies, but devotees soon clothe Green Tara in sequined garments and jewels, obscuring the purpose of her nakedness. She is one of two Taras, the wrathful one. The rather winsome White Tara is the personification of the tears of the Compassionate Buddha.

All very confusing? Well, there are other statues you may not be allowed to see without having first received proper initiations and explanations, and this is not the place to discuss them further. The Tibetans, like the Indians, knew that one picture or symbolic sculpture can say more than a thousand words to the initiated. Many of these pictures, some quite disturbing to the Western mind, have their beginnings in the ancient Bon religion of the pre-Buddhist Tibetan people, which has been incorporated into Tibetan Buddhism. To have dispensed with such statues would not necessarily have been of benefit, nor even possible, given the lack of philosophical understanding of the uneducated classes. No compassionate form of religion takes away the accepted beliefs of a people, leaving only what they often can never come to fully understand or gain from.

Around the walls of the gompa hang bright pictures framed in damask and brocade. These are tankas or 'holy' pictures. A few are covered by a curtain, drawn aside during relevant initiations or on days connected with the deity or scene depicted. There is a strong and, for me, evocative smell of Tibetan incense in the gompa. There are flickering butter lamps (now using oil instead) and flowers, and often, before the images, small, very touching personal offerings. I once left a wedding ring and two golden earrings in the open palm of the Buddha's statue there. Each statue has seven brass (or other material) bowls before it, filled daily right to the very brim with clean water, representing seven traditional offerings to the Buddhas.

During certain rituals or pujas, there are tables piled high with cakes, fruit and sweets as offerings. These are shared and eaten during the middle part of the puja (after the ceremonial offering to the Buddha) with hot spiced and buttered tea. Those observing Precepts (see chapter 1) will, of course, not eat their share until next day. The offerings have been made first to the Buddha and then shared because it is believed that all beings have the Buddha nature unrealised within, so we are, in fact, making offerings to ourselves and each other. The children of visitors and residents often run a little wild during puja or fall fast alseep. No-one is disturbed by them. Pujas are religion at its most social. I once attended six in one day—exhausting and fattening! Fortunately, I was living in a very cold climate and my shivering in an unheated cell soon burned up the excess fuel.

THERAVADIN TEMPLES

Theravadin temples will be familiar to all who have been to South East Asia. They differ only a little from country to country. Many travellers will have seen the Emerald

Buddha in Bangkok and will be familiar with the reclin-
ing Buddha statues, as well as the very distinctive slender
Buddha figure with the pointed head-dress and the Shwe
Dagon Pagoda of Angkor Wat. The images are provided
with offerings of fruit, flowers and incense by laypeople.
Monks really use their begging bowls for just that
purpose, and the food they do not need is offered at the
temple to those in need. In Australia and other Western
countries, the bowl is now a symbol reminding one not
to be self-indulgent. I, for one, should keep mine where
I can't avoid seeing it when sweet things are on the
menu.

The temples are also schools. Buddhism was the first
religion to offer secular education in the temples, usually
for boys (girls being taught at home). In some countries,
a man may become a monk for any length of time that
suits him and, in Theravadin countries, many spend at
least one period of their lives as a monk. Boys often
spend their school holidays as monks. The little monks
one sees in South East Asia, Tibet, Nepal and India may
not necessarily go on to take life vows.

There are no Theravadin nuns as such, but instead
shaven-headed women in white robes, many of whom
are widows or homeless women. They act in domestic
capacities, cleaning the temples, cooking, washing and
nursing, but are, like many Muslim women, given no
formal religious training. They live by the Precepts, do no
harm, and are therefore as Buddhist as any monk. In the
West there are now some Theravadin sects that do offer
their nuns the same religious instruction as that given the
monks. Chislehurst Theravadin Monastery in England
comes to mind. In fact, there is a growing movement
amongst Buddhist women worldwide to have the

Theravadin hierarchy allow the reintroduction of full ordination for women, which had been gradually phased out by the monks during the rise to power and importance of the individual monasteries of the Theravadin sects following the end of King Asoka's reign.

THE ZEN TEMPLE

A Zen temple has an innate neatness and simplicity so dear to the ordered mind. Yet Zen itself can appear at times, to some, as sheer chaotic madness. To be in the throes of an unsolved koan is to feel oneself on the verge of lunacy. Great! We are on the way to the answer—or not—as the case may be. A koan is a question designed to break through a too-rigid type of thinking and reasoning.

In the Zen meditation hall, meditators kneel on cushions in rows, facing each other across the open floor space, similar to Tibetan custom. Everything is understated. There is little to distract one—except perhaps the pain of cramped legs and an aching back, or the shock of a rap across the shoulders, administered by the disciplinarian monk (or nun) if the meditator's spine bends or head droops. The word Zen comes from the Sanskrit 'dyana', through the Chinese 'chan' to 'zen', and simply means 'meditation'.

A short extract paraphrased from the sutra of Hui Neng, Sixth Chan Patriarch, will best illustrate the method of Zen. Hui Neng (638–713 AD), later to become the Sixth Buddhist Patriarch of China, was the son of a Buddhist government official who had ben dismissed from his post and had died during his son's infancy. As soon as he was old enough to take the burden from his mother's shoulders, Hui Neng had to work hard to support his mother and himself. He became a wood seller, and received his education at his mother's knee and wherever else he could. He was supposed at that time to be semi-literate only, which is debatable.

One day, after delivering some wood, he heard a man in the street reciting a sutra of the Lord Buddha. It was the *Diamond Sutra* (*Vajraschedika*—one of the main Buddhist texts). He immediately grasped its meaning and was enlightened. If one has studied the sutra well and puzzled over it for years, understanding its message most certainly *can* come to one instantaneously.

Hui Neng, though allegedly semi-literate, had always been a deep thinker. He soon had the good fortune to be given a gift of money by one who saw his worth, and was advised to go to the monastery of the Fifth Patriarch. He gave his mother the money and went to the monastery in the hope of further education in the dharma. The Patriarch saw immediately that Hui Neng was already enlightened but showed him no favour, in order to shield him from jealousy—especially from the head monk, Shen Hsiu, who expected to be chosen as the next Patriarch. In order to examine the true state of the wisdom of Shen Hsiu as a candidate, the Fifth Patriarch asked all the monks to write a stanza on their understanding of Essence of Mind. He knew that only Shen Hsiu would attempt this challenge, as the other monks were afraid to compete with one whom they considered so much more learned than themselves.

Afraid to offer his stanza directly to the Patriarch, Shen Hsiu crept out at night with a lamp and, on the wall of the south corridor where the Patriarch would be sure to see it next morning, wrote the following stanza:

Our body is the Bodhi tree
And our mind a mirror bright.

Carefully we wipe them, hour by hour
And let no dust alight.

Sutra of Hui Neng, (tr. Wong Moulam)

On reading this, the Patriarch knew for sure that Shen Hsiu was not yet enlightened, but he praised the stanza and left it there to help those at or below Shen Hsiu's level of understanding.

Hui Neng heard about the stanza, even though he had spent most of his eight months at the monastery pounding rice in the kitchen. He asked a boy to show it to him, as he had never been in that section of the building. A visiting official was present and at Hui Neng's request, read the poem to him. Hui Neng surprised those present by saying he had a stanza and would like someone to write it for him, which the visitor did. This was the stanza:

There is no Bodhi tree
Nor stand of a mirror bright
Since all is void [empty of inherent existence]
Where can the dust alight?

Sutra of Hui Neng (tr. Wong Moulam)

There is of course much more to the autobiography of Hui Neng, but the difference in understanding between those two stanzas shows how Zen gets immediately to the point of the foundation of Buddhist philosophy. Zen stories make delightful reading for some, but can seem unfuriatingly obscure to others.

I still recall my own reaction to the first piece of Zen literature I ever read: infuriation! 'Why the hell can't they just say what they mean?' I fumed. Then, like most

students of the dharma, I studied and puzzled and meditated until I was thoroughly fed up and put it aside for
quite some time. It was not until much later that the
penny dropped, as the saying goes.

My inability to understand was due in part to my own
unimaginative mind—too rational and too pedantic—and
in part to my lack of a proper teacher. I was jumping in
without having learned to swim, even to dog-paddle. I had
wanted to see everything from every side, from every practical point of view. Quite suddenly I realised there was
nothing to see. There was no such thing as a bodhi tree, no
such thing as a mirror bright or otherwise. All conditioned
phenomena are, by definition, without inherent existence.

FINDING THE TEACHER

So, as we have seen, these are the three *main* types of
Buddhist religion we are likely to come in contact with,
though it is worthwhile to note that there are many 'sects'
that have far less to do with the teachings of Buddha than
with (a) the charisma of a leader and (b) the credulity
or emotional and psychological needs of that leader's
followers. In some cases no harm is done, but we have seen
in the past few years, in the actions of various cults, that
many people can be led into performing horrors because
of indiscriminate acceptance of another's instruction
without analysing for themselves what is being taught.
Sadly, those so influenced seem incapable of thinking
clearly.

In Buddhism, one is told to take the greatest care in
seeking a guru (teacher). One is warned to be completely
satisfied that this person can be trusted with one's very

life—and that they are competent to teach what one seeks to learn. It is nothing short of astonishing to see the sort of person to whom some would entrust their lives.

Nowadays there are people who set themselves up as gurus of what is called 'crazy wisdom'. If you are a 'disciple', be sure to take great care to apply the advice given above when choosing a guru. 'Crazy wisdom' is one of the modern if-it-feels-good-do-it movements. That mode of behaviour *could* be trusted in one of irreproachable character, but in the hands of an unscrupulous or merely ignorant charismatic person it may lead to disaster. It is sad that so many people need, or believe they need, someone to lean on, someone to cling to as a sort of life raft. Until we learn that no-one can 'save' us but ourselves, we will be prey to false teachers and teachings. We need other people for many reasons, including the pleasure of their company, but if we expect someone or something else to solve all our problems, we will never gain the strength and wisdom leading to peace of mind and to whatever fortifies us or constitutes happiness for us as individuals.

4

BUDDHIST MONASTICISM

How does it work and what type of person is attracted to such a life? Why are some Westerners attracted?

❧

MONASTICISM: WHAT AND WHY?

The Sangha, that collective body of Buddhists usually known as monks (bhikkhus) and nuns (bhikkhunis), lamas, gurus, Theras (Theravadin masters), masters, initiates, priests, priestesses and so on, are those who have received ordination at the hands of the previously ordained from an unbroken lineage. The Buddhist Sangha is probably the oldest known functioning monastic tradition. Like all things, it has evolved from simplicity to complexity with the passing of time.

91

Originally the Sangha consisted of those wandering
ascetics who, having understood the teachings of Sakyamuni Buddha, decided to become active followers so
they could continue to hear him and be able to question
him face to face when clarification seemed necessary.
The very first few—those who had already spent many
years investigating philosophical and experiential beliefs
before hearing the Buddha's dharma—were in a position
to fully and quickly grasp the meaning of the teachings,
and they were then sent out by the Buddha to teach those
who wished to listen. It is important here to point out
that the Buddha's first disciples were not what we in the
West understand as 'missionaries'. Their object was not
to 'convert' anyone but to speak to those who wished to
listen. Little had changed in this respect up to the present
day. Buddhists do not seek out possible 'converts' but
wait for those with enough interest to ask the questions
that show 'where they are at'. Only then can the 'signposts' be of any use to them.

At first there were no monasteries. The Sangha was
made up of wanderers—the 'homeless ones'. The climate
in north-eastern India permitted outdoor living except
during the three- or four-month monsoon season, and for
that time there were caves and temporary shelters available. Being 'homeless ones', however, did not mean they
were penniless vagrants. On the contrary, most were well
educated, from 'good' homes, often with wealthy, even
princely, backgrounds. Being homeless meant simply
that, having done one's family duty, one had renounced
the comforts and benefits of domestic and business life,
and now wished to seek the 'truth' regarding the fundamental principles of existence. This was the accepted
custom of the time. Doing one's family duty included

marrying, producing at least one heir and providing for the care of wives and children, as well as parents if they had not already set out on their own quest.

Travel was on foot and for the 'seekers' it was often dangerous due to dacoits (bandits) and wild animals. Finding food, however, was not a problem. Fruit grew everywhere and such was the respect felt by the 'at homes' for those prepared to give up domestic comforts to seek wisdom that giving sustenance to such people was looked upon as 'merit', because the giver's contribution was seen as increasing knowledge and spiritual development for the good of all. This was the social climate into which Siddhartha Gautama, the Buddha, was born and lived for more than eighty years. This was the society from which his personal followers came.

The Buddha, at first, asked only that his followers, now a permanent group, keep the Five Precepts: no killing, no stealing, no telling lies, no unlawful or abnormal sexual conduct (celibacy for Sangha members), and no intoxication from drink or drugs. Later, in order to curb vain competition, he asked that jewellery not be worn, nor rich clothing, nor elaborate hairstyles (bejewelled and beflowered top-knots and rich turbans). It was self-evident that a person taken up with unnecessary personal adornment could not seriously be intent on listening to what the Buddha was teaching.

Women were part of the Sangha from the earliest days. Traditionally, Buddha's stepmother (his deceased mother's sister, number two wife to his father and mother of the wicked Davida) was the first of her sex to be accepted. Suspect is the warning attributed to the Buddha that the admission of women would mean the demise of the Sangha within 500 years. This is possibly a monkish addition of later date. The Buddha praised the wisdom of many of the nuns. Quite often, husband and wife would be amongst the followers and this led, in some cases, to the need for more rules, as interference, no matter how well-intended on the part of one or other spouse, was not conducive to the harmony, peace and quiet necessary for celibacy, study and contemplation.

At first the Sangha consisted of groups of both men and women wandering in the parks and forests with their teacher, then later living together in temporary dwellings offered by laypeople. As time went on, it became possible for each sex to have its own buildings or monasteries, run by a few monks or nuns. Because monks at that time were often the better educated, nuns were advised to seek teachings from them, unless there were 'realised' persons among them, fit to instruct, especially during the monsoon period when travel for teachers and students became impossible. This period became known as the Rains Retreat, when all the best interpreters of the teachings were gathered together. That gathering of monks and nuns still happens, but it has become difficult for many because of migration and the need for a master to be available in the capacity of teacher. The Rains Retreat is the most suitable and convenient time for ordinations, which require the presence of a great number of fully ordained Sangha members to be in the same place at the same time.

MONASTIC RULES

With the growth of numbers and more settled living conditions for the Sangha, more 'rules' became necessary. It was not the Buddha's way to give orders. Instead he gave advice in accordance with the presented difficulty. Often legal matters regarding gifts needed clarification, as did matters such as safety during travel, especially where women were concerned, and what to do in the case of a member's gross misconduct or dishonesty. Before he died, the Buddha gave permission for changes to be made (where such were found necessary) in all but the most important rules. However, fear of throwing the baby out with the bathwater, plus later additions made according to arising circumstances, have left us with 227 rules and vows for fully ordained monks and 248 for fully ordained nuns. The difference in the number of rules is because of the different needs of women and their need for protection during travel. Many rules are mere 'splits' and repetitions. The greater number for nuns does not mean greater restrictions. In many cases, the rules concerning other times, and Indian legalities and customs, cannot be strictly adhered to in modern society. *The spirit behind the words counts most*, as the Buddha often reminded his followers. There are other rules and vows of a more religious nature related to initiations, mainly in the Mahayana sects.

The ritual stages of entry into the Sangha could be described as postulant, novice and fully ordained. The Tibetan Tradition differs slightly because the full-ordination lineage ritual for women never reached Tibet, and therefore Tibetan novices take thirty-six vows and must seek elsewhere if they wish to become fully ordained bhikkhunis. The same applies to Western women with Tibetan novice ordination, but there is no obligation to do so.

It is not absolutely necessary, and for some it is not

possible, to live full-time in monasteries. Many do from choice, some from necessity. For others, circumstances give greater opportunity to share the teachings with those who choose to enquire by living 'in the world'. These are the 'wandering' monks and nuns. As long as one lives within one's vows, one is still a member of the Sangha. Novice and fully ordained Sangha members live the same life in the monasteries except for certain rituals, which are attended only by the fully ordained, and the highest ordination ceremonies, when only the fully ordained and the candidates are present all the time.

Buddhist monastic life is divided into three parts. These are work, study and ritual. For all the Buddha's warnings against reliance on rituals as a path to enlightenment, ritual has, in many instances, become more than half of monastic activity. It can be observed in certain cultures that the populace gladly support the monasteries in return for strict, regular rituals being carried out by the monks and/or nuns. Thus the world is kept on an even keel and the gods, ghosts and spirits placated!

RITUALS AND RITES

In the Buddha teachings ritual and ceremony are not forbidden or denigrated (except regarding living sacrifice). If people want or need ritual (a very basic desire throughout human existence—and, in some cases, ritual is all they are psychologically capable of accepting), Buddhism does not deny it to them. From a purely philosophical point of view, who can say that ritual and ceremony may not be the first step, for some, toward greater awareness of what *is*—the first step toward enlightenment?

For people of such cultures there is much peace of mind to be found in knowing that a dedicated body of sincere, religiously educated, renouncing persons is taking care of everyone's spiritual wellbeing. By supporting the Sangha, the supporter gains 'merit' both to be credited in a future incarnation and affording the best protection possible in the present one.

Those officiating at daily rituals are not necessarily priests. There are no 'priests' in monastic Buddhism. Some cultures, such as Japanese Zen sects, do have monks or ex-monks taking the teaching and celebratory role amongst the people, for the purpose of instruction in the dharma, and for birth, marriage and death ceremonies and so on. These 'priests' often marry. Some live in the temple precincts, others in more private dwellings. This type of work is not, strictly speaking, a Buddhist Sangha function, but a cultural one.

Monastic Buddhism reached its greatest era of influence during the reign of Indian Emperor Asoka in the third century BC, who, after many years of bloody but successful conquest, became sickened by the slaughter and wastage of war. He embraced Buddhist precepts and encouraged his people to follow his example. The greater part of India became Buddhist.

King Asoka sent teachers of the Buddha's ideas as far as Libya and Cyrenaica and the teachings reached China and South East Asia within a short time of Buddha's death.

For monks and nuns great university monasteries such as Nalanda, dedicated to the study of Buddhist philosophy, flourished throughout the country. In the monasteries, a great deal of organisation became necessary, as happens whenever large numbers of people are permanently gathered. Under royal patronage, Buddhism became the state religion. Many Brahmins were 'converted' and became members of the Sangha, out of either conviction or expediency. Whatever their reasons, with them came many of their Brahmin beliefs, customs and even rituals. The Brahmin (and Hindu) influence can still be traced in many current Mahayana beliefs, practices and philosophical conclusions, albeit somewhat changed, and in those sects practising the Tantric tradition. For celibate sects, the physical observances of Indian Tantra (Bhakti/Bhakta) practices have been spiritualised and have become mental yoga rather than physical yoga. Tantra is so specialised that it requires much explanation by a qualified teacher, preferably one who has reached the standard of master of their particular discipline.

CELIBACY

The rule of celibacy in early Buddhism was not due to the view that sexual activity was 'sinful', 'dirty', unimportant or shameful, but for the simple, obvious reason that sexual activity (a) is lacking in *lasting* satisfaction and is therefore a *recurring* desire; and (b) distracts the mind from the intense concentration required in order to reach enlightenment in the shortest possible time, which, after all, is or should be the purpose of becoming a monastic in the first place.

Some extremely off-putting exercises have been developed. They are meant to help the would-be celibate, but they have given rise to the popular belief that Buddha hated women, that he despised sex, and that Buddhism is some kind of Eastern Puritanism. Nothing could be further from the true teachings of the Enlightened One. In the *Book of Graduate Sayings*, Volume III, page 56, the Buddha, speaking on the subject of the difficulties of celibacy for Sangha members, had this to say:

> Monks, I see no other single form so enticing,
> so desirable, so intoxicating, so distracting, such a
> hindrance to the winning of unsurpassable peace from
> effort—that is to say, monks, as a woman's form.

The exhortation goes on to suggest the exercise of seeing the desirable one as a skin bag full of pus, blood, bones, phlegm, urine, faeces and so on. Similar exercises apply also for nuns when celibacy becomes difficult for them.

Celibacy is not universal in Buddhist monasteries. In certain non-celibate Mahayana sects, especially those practising Tantra, certain monks, as we would say, 'marry'. They take a religiously aware permanent consort, who participates in ritual practice as an equal opposite. This book is not the place for deeper explanations of a much misunderstood spiritual practice, which owes much to ancient Hindu practices.

Buddhist monks and nuns are not (or should not be) suppressing their sexuality, or even sublimating it. What they do is strive to understand the forces involved and use them for ends different from unappeasable, short-term, bodily gratification. They do not dispute or denigrate the normal practices of laypeople. Quite often the case with individual monks and nuns is: 'Been there, done that, and don't need to keep on doing it any longer.' There is little that can be so potentially explosive or unpleasant as a sexually suppressed monastic—of any religion. In Buddhist practice, one does not suppress one's appetites, whether for food, comfort, sexual activity, desire for recognition or anything else; instead one seeks to understand how these desires arise, why they arise, and how they can be made use of as tools, rather than being hindrances if they cannot easily be eliminated.

MONASTICS

The reasons for entering a monastery are as numerous as the candidates who enter. In an established monastery, postulants can be observed, their behaviour evaluated and they can be examined orally about their understanding. They can be educated step by step until, having reached a certain level (regardless of the time taken to do so), they can be ordained novices and the process continued, for however long it takes (at least two years), until they are considered—by the abbot, abbess, master, geshè, lama, guru, entire community or whoever is in charge—to be ready for highest ordination. This is, of course, the ideal. However, in today's climate of suppression and persecution of monasticism in many parts of the world, this straightforward graduated path is no longer always possible. Monasteries and temples have been closed or destroyed, and the monks and nuns dispersed or killed. It is taking time to re-establish the monasteries and temples, to educate the necessary teachers and to make sure the direct-from-Buddha lineage of ordination is genuine and available.

Some sects, in order to develop new monastic groups, scatter the seeds of ordination almost on demand in the hope that some will germinate and grow. Highest ordination is a lifelong commitment, but being a postulant or novice lasts as long as the candidate wishes. The same applies for initiation vows given in Mahayana rituals, although these too should be lifelong. Within the monastic community one should keep Vinaya (monastic) rules or face expulsion by the community. This is no different from the practice of any social or religious community.

Buddhism is not what Westerners think of as an organised religion. As I've explained there is no Pope, no Archbishop of Canterbury. Contrary to popular belief, His Holiness Tenzin Gyatso, fourteenth Dalai Lama, is not the 'Pope' of Buddhism. He is simply, through circumstances not of his making (and his own personality) the most widely known Buddhist today. Every Buddhist country has its own most revered religious 'leaders', as does every group of students of religious Buddhism. Guru, lama and similar names mean only teacher. A teacher is the leader of a group of followers.

There is no 'higher authority' passing down rules and regulations pertaining to the beliefs and practices of all Buddhists. There are new interpretations and new translations of religious and philosophical Buddhist texts being presented almost regularly—this is the serious student's good fortune—but the basic teachings do not change, nor does one's responsibility for one's choice of action or reaction—one's own karma.

The Demise of Indian Monasticism
By the eleventh century AD, the Buddhist Sangha in India had almost ceased to exist. It had been deteriorating for some centuries for historical reasons. The two main causes of its decline were (a) the weakening effect of ideas brought in by Brahmin philosophers; and (b) persecution of Buddhists by Muslims, including the

destruction of universities and monasteries, and the killing or dispersion of the Sangha, as is what happens all over the world when one culture overcomes another by conquest of arms. It is fortunate that long before all this happened, the Buddhist dharma had been introduced to and revered in many other lands. The texts had been written earlier in Pali and Sanskrit and many of those, with additional philosophical treatises of later dates, were translated into other languages. Tibet, in particular, has or had a treasure trove of such texts, many still not translated. In view of the recent destruction wreaked on the monasteries in that country, we shall never know what has been lost, although the monks who escaped took with them all the texts they could carry out. It is ironic that Buddhism, the religion/philosophy of non-violence, should have been disseminated and often eventually saved indirectly by violence. If the Dalai Lama, his tutors and followers had not been forced to leave their home-lands the spread of knowledge of at least *Tibetan* Buddhism would have been left to a few individuals with enough interest to attempt to teach it. Hinduism grew out of Brahmanic/Vedic philosophy and it would be difficult, if not impossible today to find a Buddhist community in India which is not a recent re-introduction.

The coming into being of the Buddhist Sangha was a gradual development. This is seen clearly in the slow accretion of rules as they became necessary to the smooth running of organised groups. The way it was done, according to the history of the Vinaya, was that, as a difficulty or dispute arose, it was, initially, reported to the Buddha and, if it seemed likely to recur, a rule was made. If the Buddha was not available, a senior disciple (an arahant) would make a rule for the given situation.

Eventually, as we have seen, there were 227 rules for monks and 248 for nuns.

The Vinaya was one of the very first Buddhist texts to be translated into Western languages and formed the basis of Western 'understanding' of Buddhism. So the assumption grew that *all* Buddhists live (or ought to live) a life strictly in accordance with monastic rules. It was not understood that the Vinaya developed slowly and out of then-prevailing circumstances for a specific purpose. Lay Buddhists keep the Five Precepts and on occasion eight. Any other rules they place upon their own behaviour, whether skilful or unskilful, are their own choice and responsibility.

VEGETARIANISM

Vegetarianism in Buddhist practice was a development from the precept not to kill. It is written in the texts that the Buddha said: 'Eat what is offered but do not ask that something be killed for you'. As the monks and nuns went out each morning with their begging bowls, they did not even look at what was placed there by laypeople and most certainly would not have made specific requests or rejected anything offered. The food was taken back to the group and shared by all as the only meal of the day. The food was part of whatever was the normal diet of the people. Once it became widely known that Buddhists took the Five Precepts quite sincerely, a sensitive person would refrain from offering flesh, even if it happened to be part of their own diet.

Tibetan monastics have always eaten meat when it was available, their climate making a full variety of vegetable foods difficult. Keeping good health to the best of one's ability is necessary for the rigours of the climate and their religious practices. In warm climates, fruit, vegetables and cereals are an adequate diet.

WHY BE A MONK OR NUN?

What would direct a normal person toward a life regulated by a set of more than 200 rules or vows? To begin with, what is a 'normal' person? It is easier to say what is not normal than to clearly define what is normal. There are the abnormal and also the super-normal and the supra-normal. It is not the strictly normal/average/ordinary we must look for, because all psychological types can be found amongst monastics as well as among lay followers of Buddhism. Here we must deal with the type of people who, for whatever reason, wish to renounce 'worldly' life, for however long it suits them, in order to discover something about the 'self' or about existence. The following impressions arise from personal experience and observations.

Initial interest in the teachings of Buddha Sakyamuni is often triggered by awakening to the fact that one's life is lacking in clarity, in permanent happiness, in peace of mind, in hope, in purpose, in self-discipline. This awakening may have any number of triggers, which—no matter how petty some may seem to others—are of prime importance at that time to that person, possibly seen as the most epic happenings in all of human history. This awareness may come through having too little of what is desired or from over-indulging leading to revulsion. One may awaken from a feeling of ecstacy or from despair.

One may awaken from one's perceived good fortune or from sorrow or loss—the causes and conditions are infinite. It may be a simple matter of realising one is on the 'wrong' path, travelling aimlessly or to a place one has no real wish to go to.

There is often, at first, an unfocused seeking for reasons why things are as they are; where one went 'wrong'; what, if anything, one can do about it; or for someone who can help. This seeking may be conscious or unconscious. There must be very few people in the world who are really fully content with their condition in life. Even the yogi-to-be, at a certain stage of the 'quest', is, in fact, questing or striving or grasping for enlightenment. Only one whom we call a 'Buddha' is completely free of grasping/desiring. So one who initially becomes interested in the dharma is a 'spiritually' hungry person, actively trying to find a cure for the ills of personal existence and the existence of all sentient beings.

Why does the seeker desire a personal 'cure'? The answers are as many as there are seekers, but they can be, very loosely, gathered into certain categories. To begin somewhere, there is the person who, having lived a full life and having come to understand the ultimate lack of lasting satisfaction, or who has simply had enough (has 'been there, done that'), has come to feel there is more to life than personal gratification. Altruism arises— a desire to do something to help other sentient beings find happiness and freedom from the seeming chaos of their lives. There can also be that fierce desire to know the fundamental principles of existence.

Another type of person, whose life has been a complex muddle, a series of self-excavated potholes on the road of life, and who is at the point of greatest muddle, comes

to realise there has to be a better way to live, with more
to it than muddle and the often awful consequences of
muddle.

There are those who feel that human relationships
(family, friends or romantic partners) have let them
down, so they seek a non-human 'relationship'—a guard-
ian, a guide, 'one' higher than the human or animal, who
will give them unchanging love and appreciation of the
qualities they know they possess. They seek a father/
mother/lover/friend figure of unchanging constancy, love
and acceptance. This is possibly the largest group of
'seekers'.

Another type is the would-be live-in hermit—one who
longs for a quiet place, not a lonely hermitage, but a
place where they can be supported in a non-intrusive
way while they try to sort out conflicting emotions and
ideas, a place where one can do no harm to others and
where one would be free from the distractions of personal relationships and responsibilities.

The above types may or may not be religiously
minded, but of those who are, because of their particular
culture, there is (a) the person who seeks personal
enlightenment first in order to know how best to then
be of help to others; and (b) the person who would like
to be able to help *all* others, before themselves, to enlightenment—the would-be bodhisattva of Mahayana
Buddhism.

There is the type of person who, feeling a strong need,
actively seeks discipline imposed by an authority they
respect, or even hold in awe. This person often feels great
pleasure and release in being cheerfully submissive to
monastic rules.

In South East Asian Buddhist countries, there are many

whose marriage has been ended by death or desertion, especially poor widows, as well as refugees with no other path open to them, who know there is a place for them in a monastery.

I am not qualified to give a clear idea of the psychological make-up of myself or any other person, but I offer the above descriptions on the basis of having met such people in lay or monastic life. No account is given of the mentally unbalanced or psychologically disturbed, who also may be sincere 'seekers' at some time.

A person who has, for whatever reason, become aware of the need to change their way of life and who then comes into contact in some way with the dharma will become, most likely, a lay follower or seek entry into a monastic community at the level of upasika or upasaka (a man or woman who wishes to dwell as a monastic for a short time).

There are two other types who account for large numbers of monastics: the devotional and the superstitious. The first is the most common of all monastics and lay followers; the second is also common and lives a life in fear of offending unseen 'powers'. For the first type, ritual is a pleasure with its colour, its familiarity and the feeling it gives that one is able to offer something to the object of one's devotion. For the second type, ritual becomes an absolute necessity to prevent the sky falling or experiencing a 'bad' rebirth.

Because of the variety of people involved, one is urged to enquire very carefully into the thinking (and actions) of the person one chooses as a guru or teacher, called (in dharma) one's spiritual friend.

As stated previously, no vows below highest ordination need be for life. The late, revered (especially by his

Western students) Tibetan Lama Thubten Yeshè, when
giving postulant vows to two young women seeking
novice vows from His Holiness the Dalai Lama through
Lama's intercession, gently questioned the strength of
their commitment. Although *they* were sure, Lama was
not so sure, but gently and kindly, as his wisdom always
was, murmured: 'Better a nun for a short time than never
at all.' Lama was right. Neither remained a nun for more
than a year, but both learned a great deal during that
time.

The accepted way for a monastic to leave the order is
to 'give back the robes and vows' to the one who gave
them, or to the abbot or abbess of the nearest monastery.
By observing the courtesy of this method, one does not
suffer guilt for breaking vows and will receive blessings
and good advice from one's teacher.

In some places and in some people there is a certain
animosity towards monastics. The shaven head of a Buddhist monk or nun often draws unpleasant reactions,
especially if the monastic is Western and female. Some
men seem to feel the nun is rejecting them all. Some
women feel that the nun is rejecting as unimportant
all that makes them desirable and their chosen way of
life. Monks, on the other hand, seem to inspire respect
from both sexes. It's an interesting psychological
phenomenon.

What appears strange to a layperson—the robes and
the shaven head—is perfectly normal in the monastery
situation and frees the monastic from the necessity of
dressing the hair every day, while the wearing of the
robes removes the necessity of thinking about what to
wear and what goes with what. Even so, little vanities
can still arise: the colour and cloth of a robe, the most

regularly denuded skull, the number of 'burns' and so on.

The matter of monasticism in Buddhism is, in the most elementary terms, simply a way of living which, for a certain type of person, seems to offer the best conditions for the undistracted concentration on whatever it is they hope to gain from the Buddhist philosophy/religion. It is a purely personally motivated decision, with no coercion involved at any level and no rules, other than those of the Vinaya, to be followed by the monastic. As Buddhism is based on non-violence and universal compassion, there is absolutely no cause for fear, by anyone, of monastic practices. A large group of robed monastics may appear as a many-headed automaton, but this is not the case at all. Each monk and nun retains their independence and, far from being drilled to obey orders, is encouraged to continually, as the Buddha himself advised, investigate, investigate, investigate. It is monks who seem to take best to total discipline; nuns are more 'unruly'.

The non-monastic general public need have no fear of being religiously influenced by Buddhist monastics. Once they realise that monks and nuns are, as we all are, human beings seeking only to find whatever it may be that means 'happiness' for themselves and for all suffering beings, they would find in them only kindness and a willingness to be supportive.

5

MEDITATION

How, When, Where and Why?

৵৻

To begin with, it needs to be clearly understood that Buddhist meditation does not mean going into a trance. A person in a trance state is not aware of what is going on around them, which accounts for the amazing feats of a physical nature that one sees performed by certain yogis. During Buddhist meditation, one becomes more—not less—aware of what is going on because the mind is not distracted by chasing after every sensation and thought. Awareness becomes clearer but at the same time completely unattached or freed from clinging.

We tend to assume that in the waking state we are fully

aware. What we do not realise is how much we put between ourselves and real awareness. We constantly seek distraction with radio, television, newspapers, films and so on, and with endless worry, so that something occupies our minds. We are becoming accustomed to being constantly 'entertained'. We do anything—ANY-THING—rather than be aware of the way things really are and what, out of it all, is important to us. What is important is that the limited information that comes in through our sometimes flawed senses is distorted by our perceptions and past conditioning. We need to stop following the mind's activities to allow ourselves to become truly aware of what is going on. Then we will be able to act more skilfully on behalf of ourselves and others.

Buddhist meditation (certain Tantric practices excluded) is not achieved with pleasant sounds and comforting mental pictures of oneself in delightful surroundings with imaginary guides, with all one's problems put aside for the time being. These practices have their uses for the immediate relief from excess stress, but remain only temporary escapes, as are all such entertainments. These popular forms of meditation are another means of not getting down to the nitty-gritty of investigating the reality of a situation.

THE CONTROLLED MIND

So much for what Buddhist meditation is *not*. For what it *is*, we need to go to the correct translation of the word 'bhāvanā'. The English word 'meditation' was the nearest early translators were able to come to the meaning of the Pali/Sanskrit word. Bhāvanā means development or culture—mental development, mental culture. This is mental yoga, as distinct from purely physical yoga (which the Buddha found did not lead to enlightenment). Buddhist meditation develops mind control, control of one's *own* mind.

Why is mind control so important? Because where the mind goes, the body tends to follow, for good or ill. A controlled mind can be directed skilfully while an uncontrolled mind is full of 'drunken-monkey chatter' and mistaken perceptions leading to unskilful behaviour and unnecessary suffering. A controlled mind can absorb more clearly the overall picture. The uncontrolled mind is too full of narrow concerns to get more than momentary glimpses of reality: of dependent origination, of the emptiness of inherent existence of phenomena, of the reasons for lack of happiness in everyday life.

Popular forms of meditation are grasped at eagerly, because everyone is seeking a way out of suffering. Let anyone advertise offering such a way and they will soon acquire a following. I recall seeing in a Nepalese town a notice that read: 'ENLIGHTENMENT GUARANTEED, $600'. The 'teacher' made a nice living and was never short of 'disciples'. There are always people who feel cast adrift in life and who seek an answer to the old question, 'Is this all there is to life?'

Buddhist meditation (bhāvanā) is of most use to those who have arrived at a point where they have become aware of a need to learn how to see more clearly what life is about and why events occur as they do. They have begun to feel a need to live life in such a way as to do less harm to themselves and others. These are the people who have the potential to gain most from Buddhist meditation.

WHEN TO MEDITATE

At first, meditate as regularly as possible. Whether one's meditation session is to be for ten minutes or an hour or more, it will bring best all-round results when one is beginning the practice if meditation is carried out at a predetermined time. The self-discipline necessary for regular practice is itself part of the preparation, or preliminaries, for meditation. This small discipline is the beginning of a more disciplined way of living, carrying within it many benefits of mental and emotional stability.

Those who become adept in the practice acquire a continuous mental state of meditation. Place or time or conditions make no difference to this state. The outward manifestations are a thoughtful (although without actual 'thought') serenity, an ability to give full attention to the moment while remaining aware of the 'big picture', and a lack of judgmental discrimination regarding all phenomena.

The adept is in a state of meditation whether sitting, standing, walking, attending to bodily needs, natural functions, or carrying on the activities necessary for livelihood. Achieving this state depends on the capability of the meditator—it is quicker for some than others, and is not gained by 'grasping' and conscious effort but by *effortless* perseverance. It is paradoxical that the Buddhist meditator is aiming at achievement without effort, the achievement of no-thing.

Many religiously minded persons, even though able to grasp the idea of a completely integrated, interconnected One (God everywhere, in all things), are nevertheless unable to see themselves as part of the One. They expend mental and emotional energy on the effort to be united with the One, which remains forever 'other', even if divine grace is granted for a union. From the Buddhist point of view, there is no 'other', only the One of which everything is part. Personal experience would give a clearer explanation than a thousand of my words could do.

Without doubt, the most productive times for meditation are early morning, noon and evening. An early morning session sets the tone for the day; a noon session, when possible, calms the morning worries and permits a clearer view of difficulties; the evening session clears the mind of extraneous concerns, leaving it to get on with sorting and solving the daily intake of impressions and permitting untroubled sleep—not a bad return for perhaps an hour-and-a-half or even half-an-hour of one's day. Practice will soon show the amazing ability of the undistracted mind to see daily problems more clearly in context than we usually see them while 'up to our necks' in them.

The question of a place in which to meditate brings up, for many, mental pictures of shady cloisters, quiet leafy groves, dim caves, deserted beaches, remote hermitages and such locations. Nice work if you can get it, of course. For the adept, the answer to the question of *where* to meditate is simply: anywhere/everywhere. For the beginner, the following advice is offered.

Choose the quietest room in your dwelling, the one in which you are least likely to be interrupted. Clear a shelf, table or chest top and set up your 'focus point'. On a clean cover, place the following: your choice of a flower, either placed in a vase or left to wither and be replaced, as a reminder of impermanence; a candlestick and candle; a bowl of clear or perfumed water; an image or picture (religious or otherwise) for the practice of one-pointed concentration, and/or anything of the above nature which you find engenders calmness or can be a subject of your very personal mental or visual focus.

Meditate on your cushion in this place regularly until you reach the point of not needing a special place. An advantage of the 'altar' or focus point is that, even when you are not involved in a session, the mere memory of that point will help to calm the mind, by mental association with the quiet of meditation.

Meditation is not a game for the attraction of attention or admiration from others. Outside of a monastery or temple, especially in a busy Western society, a person unnecessarily taking up a pose of meditation where they are sure to be noticed is often only bidding for personal attention or ego food.

In the dwelling of the average religious Buddhist, the family altar is the focus point for prayer and, in certain cultures, for paying reverence to the spirits of the ancestors, while meditation is felt to be the province of the Sangha, not exclusively, but generally. For Zen and similar types of meditation, the 'where' is simply za zen (facing the wall).

The following methods for the practice of Buddhist meditation are an amalgam taken from the practices of various sects, but investigation will prove the basic methods to be very similar.

Although, for rituals, some sects kneel and some sit in as near to the lotus position as possible, for the individual, the correct and best but not the only position for meditation is 'cross-legged'. There are very good reasons for this which will be explained with several basic methods of meditation.

The preliminaries to meditation will differ slightly according to the religious beliefs and practices of the meditator (whether meditation takes place in public, as in the temple, or in the home) and with the preferences of the individual. In the home, step one would be, for the morning session, cleaning and arranging the altar. The image, if used, is cleaned; the cover, if used, changed; fresh flowers arranged; offerings placed; and candles or lamps lit. These actions are seen, in themselves, as offerings of respect and gratitude for the memory of the Enlightened One and his teachings, and for the wellbeing of all sentient beings.

Next, the devotee bows low to the altar or, in some sects, prostrates before it. Tibetans join their palms, thumbs between them (the thumbs represent a wish-fulfilling gem that is mentally offered whenever this gesture is used, even in the folded hands namastè greeting), on top of the head, at the throat and at the heart level, then drop to their knees and touch the forehead to the floor, doing this three times. They may fully prostrate by stretching the body face-down with arms extended. Other sects may kneel and touch forehead to floor, with hands palm-up as a gesture of lifting the Buddha's feet from the ground. These gestures are mainly cultural or personal preferences. One is, of course, shoeless in a temple and necessarily so if one is to meditate in a cross-legged position.

These preliminary practices may sound rather cut-and-dried, slightly mechanical when written, but the meditator gets as much as they give in mental attitude. Meditative states are not 'free'; as in the rest of life, one gets nothing for nothing. The more one is sincere and the more willing to persevere, the more one will 'get' from one's practice.

As previously stated, the best position for meditation is as near as one can manage to the lotus position. For long-legged or elderly people and for some other Westerners, this position can be difficult. The lotus position requires the legs to be bent at the knee and crossed, right leg in front, left foot sole-up on the right thigh; right foot sole-up on left thigh. If this cannot be managed the half-lotus is quite satisfactory. This position still allows the knees to touch the floor if one adjusts the back of the meditation cushion to the appropriate height.

The spine should be straight without stiffness, head bent slightly forward, shoulders relaxed, arms bent, right hand palm-up on left in the lap, arms a little away from the sides for the sake of ventilation, thumbs touching. Eyes may be closed or, if half-open, the gaze may be directed at a point in front, along the line of the nose, or alternatively it may be directed just below eye level, which is also a good height for the visual focus point. The lips should be relaxed—not pressed together, not sagging apart. The tongue should lightly touch the back of the upper teeth. One breathes through the nostrils to prevent the mouth from becoming dry.

This position lessens the amount of effort placed on the heart and lungs for the purpose of circulation. Hands together, thumbs touching, is a way of closing the energy circuits of the body. When first using this position, the beginner may be plagued with fleeting pains as the muscles are asked to do unaccustomed extensions or contractions. It is recommended that one does not try to ignore the discomfort but, on the contrary, should direct the mind to the trouble spot and mentally investigate it in every aspect: Where exactly is it? How deeply inside? What kind of pain is being experienced? Eventually the discomfort will ease and the muscles adapt. Fighting the discomfort will cause only more tension.

The most basic, but not necessarily the easiest, meditation practice is '**watching the breath**'. This requires the practitioner to be fully aware, without conscious thought on the matter, of the coming and going of the breath through the nostrils. While we may become aware of rapid or deeper breathing on exertion, we very rarely become aware of the breath as it continually enters and leaves the body via the nostrils, and on the skin between them and the upper lip. It is this incoming and outgoing on which we are to effortlessly concentrate. It sounds so easy that many people just cannot be bothered attempting it, thinking it possible to scale the heights of the higher meditative states without preparation. Yet that is similar to attempting to build a vast and beautiful edifice without first preparing the foundations.

While one is 'watching the breath', sounds and aromas and flashes of thought may attract the attention. One learns to let such phenomena enter and leave the awareness without following them or clinging to them. The *awareness* remains but the *grasping* does not occur. A human being cannot be *fully* aware of more than one phenomenon at a time in the early stages of meditation practice. This makes it a little easier to accomplish the 'watching the breath' exercise if one continually, on becoming aware of distraction, brings the consciousness back to the sensation of the breath entering and leaving the nostrils.

There are variations on the 'watching the breath' meditation practice, one of which is to count the inhalations or expirations up to ten, over and over again. Alternatively, one may count to ten and then back to one. The object of the exercise is to be *fully* aware of whatever one is doing.

A more complicated exercise is known as '**the nine breathings**'. One takes three breaths in and out through the right nostril, then three through the left, followed by three through both nostrils. It may be of help to block one nostril at a time until one learns to distinguish the different sensations occurring due to the slightly different internal structure of each nostril.

With these apparently simple exercises one is learning the concentration necessary for further progress. It would not be possible to achieve successful bhāvanā before learning not to be distracted by, for example, the song of a bird, the sound of a voice, traffic noises, the scent of flowers or unpleasant smells, or any of the auditory and olfactory effects of everyday life. When acquiring any skill (and highest meditation is a *learned* skill), the most important part of the training is the *basic* part. No base, no progress. No foundation, no house.

When one has learned not to grasp at external distractions, there are many subjects for basic meditation. One's own body is a most suitable subject. Begin with the skin, with all its sensations of temperature and tactile experience, then investigate each organ of the body and its function with the imagination, and, when the body has been thoroughly mentally dissected, try to imagine its emptiness of inherent existence. The awareness that all is a *connected* whole, one part relying on the others for its ability to function, and they on it, becomes apparent. This exercise is one that, when the meditator is ready, is used in the search for what we call 'I', or the soul.

Just as in the above meditations, the next step is to investigate the mind. One observes how thoughts arise and go, but one does not follow them. In the course of this practice there is often a particular thought that persists. The most persistent thought, which is often a psychological problem if it is not a daily-life problem, is then taken as a meditation subject and investigated from all angles, without emotional attachment. This investigation requires the strictest honesty regarding one's own part in the 'problem'. This type of meditation works best with guidance from a teacher at first. Once the technique is acquired, one is able to use it to gain insight into what is really happening and therefore to handle situations more skilfully. Here it is of greatest importance to learn that we are responsible for our own actions and reactions. We should come to see clearly that other people, or other circumstances, do not make us happy, sad, angry or whatever. Simply reading about all this is worthless without practice. We *choose* to react to events in a certain way, determined by our perceptions and conditioning. Too often we react without the benefit of all the necessary information available to us, because we are not aware of it or not in charge of our own emotions. Emotion clouds awareness and disturbs perceptions. No-one can 'see' a situation as it really is if they are under the control of strong emotion.

There is a common human belief that swift reaction is commendable, and it would be if it were based on what is *really* happening—on reality. The state of human relationships often shows that swift, uninformed reactions lead to disaster, to hatred and cruelty. Therefore it is surely incumbent upon us to do the best we can to gain insight into the true nature of phenomena. In relation to the above, it is worth noting that of all religious peoples, only Buddhists do not go to war in order to wipe out other religions or to impose their own beliefs, although monks and nuns have taken up arms to defend themselves and others *without* anger and being fully aware of the real purpose of their actions. In the case of those cultural Buddhists who, as in the Theravadin countries, enter monasteries for short periods as national trainees, their actions cannot be predicted or properly controlled. They are not educated in the dharma to any great degree. The aim of Buddhism, enlightenment, cannot be imposed but is a matter for individual responsibility.

Walking can be a form of meditation. In some temples and monasteries this is done single file, around the inner walls, with time kept by individual walkers striking small metal triangles and, in Vietnamese and Chinese traditions, wooden 'fishhead' drums. The pace is slow, full attention being given to the movements of the body, especially the feet and toes. This type of meditation is often accompanied by repetitive chanting. The hands are held at chest level, palm to palm, and the gaze directed at the ground about a metre ahead of one. In a temple, the monks and nuns lead in order of seniority (based on date of ordination), with laypeople following and children, if any, bringing up the rear. Knowing just where one is supposed to be in the line removes need for thought or concern in the matter. This assists in calming the mind so that full attention can be given to what one is doing at that time. Many Asian Buddhists take seniority of ordination very seriously. It is conducive to order, which contributes to the general good.

A Buddhist, whether of a religious, philosophical or ethical persuasion, has a wealth of meditation subjects to choose from and a good meditation master will often tailor a practice for an individual, taking into account where the disciple is at spiritually or what the disciple is capable of.

As we have seen, watching the breath is the basic type of meditative practice. No matter where we are, whether we're in a palace or a prison, we are breathing. The body with its functions and sensations is also ever present, as is the mind. It follows that externals such as altars and images are merely for the purpose of concentrating the attention or for bringing to mind further subjects for contemplation—or so it ought to be.

Tantric Buddhist practitioners have a wealth of intricate and colourful subjects for use in ritual and mind training. To explain these fully would require another literary work and a very experienced practitioner.

The most edifying subject for the believer in reincarnation as well as for the non-believer is **universal compassion**. In this form of meditation one imagines one is with three persons. To one's right stands the most beloved; to the left stands the most disliked, perhaps even hated or feared, person; in front stands a stranger to whom one is quite indifferent. Imagining that all of us have existed thousands of times previously as humans, as either sex and with different dispositions, one exchanges the imagined beloved for the most hated, then the one to whom one is indifferent, and for each in turn, and so on, remembering that each may have at some time been one's loving mother or father, enemy, or a person of complete indifference. To see a friend change into an enemy, a stranger become very dear or an enemy become a friend is not an uncommon experience in everyday life, whether or not there have been or will be other 'lives'.

For the practitioner who finds the idea of personal reincarnation difficult to accept, the contemplation of every sentient being, past and present, being subject to inescapable suffering of one sort or another in *this* life, is used for the nurture of compassion for all—universal compassion.

Universal compassion is not sloppy sentimentality. One is not expected to weep on the neck of the child molester or the maniacal sadist. One recognises the Buddha nature—the potential to be enlightened—within the individual while realising that whether that potential develops is up to that individual. There is ample guidance available, but the seeker will not recognise it until they are ready to do so. Universal compassion is an attitude of mind that simply recognises the 'criminal' as a fellow suffering sentient being. What to do to improve matters in such cases is problematic, but one's practice of compassion does not *necessitate* personal contact. With the mental attitude of universal compassion, one will be ever ready with real empathy and sympathy to negate, in one's own mind, desire for revenge, for 'getting even', or desire for punishment for the perceived criminal.

Universal compassion does not cause one to neglect one's own defence. As Lama Thubten Yeshè, the late revered Tibetan teacher, once said to a community persecuted by a particularly aggressive person: 'We have compassion but we are not doormats.' Not all Buddhists will turn the other cheek. One does what needs to be done without anger.

Meditation was practised before the Buddha's time, but he considered the yogic mystic states gained through Brahmanic practices as mind-produced, mind-created and mind-conditioned and not leading to full enlightenment, which is seeing things as they *really* are in the present moment. He had, during his ascetic period, tried all those methods of gaining understanding and, while he did not exclude them, he developed what is known as vipassanā or 'insight' meditation, which did lead to full enlightenment. This is true Buddhist bhāvanā (mental culture).

There are four main sections in insight meditation, dealing with firstly our bodies, secondly our feelings and sensations, thirdly the mind, and fourthly moral and intellectual subjects. It is best not to try to jump from one step to the other before mastering the previous one, for without the concentration developed in the first stage, one will not progress in the others.

It is advisable not to force oneself into long periods of practice to the point where aversion to the practice arises. Training the mind is like training an unruly animal and it is best to work gradually until the mind comes to look forward to the training sessions.

Most people live in the past, their personal past or the historical past, while they and others continually project their minds into the future, so that the present moment is disregarded, not given full attention. Meditation on insight trains one to be fully alert to the present moment, seeing it in its true relation to the past or its most probable effect on the future. By living in the past or the future, with memories or hopes and desires, we do not enjoy the present nor act skilfully in the 'now' moments of our lives. We tend to carry great loads of guilt and feelings of regret all the time, even when we have done whatever we could to remedy the results of past unskilfulness. We spend much time in wanting, in desiring, what we do not have and often have no hope of ever having. Either way, or both ways, we let the 'now' moments go by without getting any pleasure or peace from them or being aware of the possibilities the 'now' holds for us.

The initial benefits of bhāvanā are quickly achieved if one is confident and willing to persevere. One's health and daily relationships improve with the calmness and serenity induced by the practices. One becomes more aware of one's actions of body, speech and mind in relation to others and this affects their reactions to ourselves, leading to greater harmony.

All this concentration on one's actions and feelings is not for the purpose of making one self-conscious. One does not meditate with thoughts ('I am breathing in, I am breathing out', and so on). One forgets one's 'self' and loses oneself in the breathing. It becomes not 'my' breathing but simply breathing. This is, of course, how all great work is achieved; the artist, the writer, the musician, or the scientist, having learned a craft, simply does it without consciousness of self.

While investigating one's mind, one is simply aware of the 'state' of one's mind. Is it overpowered with ill-will, hatred, thoughts of revenge and so on? Is if full of compassion, clarity of understanding, contentment? The 'meditator' here is not judge and jury or severe critic deciding between right and wrong. One is the *non*-attached observer, not emotionally involved, just watching how feelings arise, 'seeing' them and watching how they pass. Not discriminating. Thoughts and feelings do not engender more thoughts and feelings about themselves. We do not worry about our worries.

Anything and everything can be used as a subject in Buddhist meditation once the practitioner has gained the ability to concentrate attention without effort. To assist in achieving this level, it is useful to take as subjects for meditation the **Five Hindrances to Progress**:

1. Lustful desires.
2. Ill-will, hatred or anger.
3. Torpor or languor.
4. Restlessness and worry.
5. Sceptical doubts.

The qualities that the Buddhist wishes to develop as aids in the progress towards enlightenment are listed as the **Seven Factors of Enlightenment**. They are:

1. Mindfulness, that is, being aware and mindful of the activities of the body, speech and mind.
2. Investigation and research into our religious, ethical and philosophical beliefs.
3. Energy and determination to carry on the above, and to finish what one begins.
4. Joy, the opposite of gloomy pessimism.
5. Relaxation, that is, not being 'stiff', physically or mentally.
6. Concentration.
7. Equanimity, that is, being able to face whatever occurs with a calm, undisturbed mind.

The Four Noble Truths (see page 11), especially the first two, if made regular, serious subjects of meditation, must in themselves bring about a much clearer understanding of existence, leading to less frustration in our lives.

There are, for the Buddhist practitioner, many other meditational subjects, traditionally a list of forty. Below are four of these, known as the **Four Sublime States**.

1. Mettā, extending unlimited, universal love to all living beings.

2. Karuna, compassion for all suffering and afflicted beings.
3. Mudita, sympathetic joy in the success, welfare and happiness of others.
4. Equanimity, that is, being able to face whatever occurs with a calm, undisturbed mind.

These are some of the aims of the practising Buddhist of whatever sect, in whatever culture. This is what really matters even when strange rituals, robes and customs may seem off-putting to the Western–Protestant–Puritan type of mind confronted with aspects of alien religious cultures. For hundreds of years since the religious Reformation movements throughout Europe, many Westerners have tended to see ritual, images and material offerings in a religious context as somehow threatening to the 'purity' of their own beliefs. If we are *sure* of our own beliefs, we should not fear the beliefs of others. Unfortunately we tend to fear what we do not understand and, worse still, fear *to* understand in case we start to question the 'truth' of our own beliefs. Even a little knowledge of others' way of viewing existence should, one would fervently hope, be the means of promoting, at the very least, tolerance.

WHY TOLERATE DIFFERENCES?

Tolerance does not require *acceptance* of another's religious beliefs and practices but simply the willingness to let others live life as they see fit and to get on with living one's own life as well as possible.

Intolerance fosters religious wars (surely the supreme

oxymoron) where one 'side' attempts to impose its own ideas by force on the other 'side', or to wipe out that side altogether, thus feeling they have 'proved' their own ideas to be the truth. If the individual is strong in their own faith, fully satisfied with the answers it gives to important questions of existence, fully satisfied it makes its followers better people doing the least harm to living beings, fully satisfied that it represents 'truth', then the question one must ask is: 'Why fight about it?' What is to be feared from another's ideas? Do we, perhaps, fear that not having fully investigated (meditated upon) the tenets of 'our' religion, the religion we *profess* to understand, we may have to ask ourselves questions we fear to ask? Questions that will show us the weakness, not necessarily of the tenets of 'our' religion, but of our own ignorance of those tenets? To admit our own ignorance is intolerable for most of us. Thus we tend to strike out at whatever threatens to expose us and our supposed truth, but without the clarity of thought that would show us that we are not defending our religion at all but our own ego, our *idea* of ourselves.

Buddhism does not attempt to prove its teachings correct, it only holds that, if you are interested, try its practices for yourself. To practise Buddhist types of meditation does not mean you automatically become a Buddhist or even need to live by Buddhist precepts. It is all a matter of personal experience, your business, or as is said in Pidgin English: 'Samting belong iu.' No-one will seek to 'enfold you in the flock'. Buddhism does not work that way. How you live your life is your own responsibility. You make your choice and accept the consequences. So there is no need to fear the influence of this 'new' religion (well, fairly new to us in this country), for its adherents do not proselytise. No Buddhist will come knocking at your door to attempt to convert you to Buddhism. It simply cannot be done. All the knowledge is available but only if you ask for it. Why should we be intolerant of so unthreatening a philosophy/ religion?

There is so much of beauty and wonder in this life and yet it is in constant danger of passing us by, never to be regained, if we do not learn to be fully aware of the 'now' moments.

For anyone interested in practising meditation there are teachers to be found at any Buddhist study centre and there are countless books on the subject available at those centres and in the religion/philosophy sections of libraries and bookshops. Initially, Buddhist meditation is not a do-it-yourself subject but requires a trusted teacher, if possible, a meditation master, to set the would-be meditator on the right path. It is most helpful to begin by immediately asking oneself: 'Why do I wish to learn to meditate and what do I expect to gain from the practice?'

To write more fully on Buddhist meditation leaves the writer open to the accusation of drifting into metaphysics, of possessing a high-flown imagination, of being a 'mystic', an 'air head'. What the meditator achieves develops stage by stage and must, of necessity, be differently experienced by each person. If an accomplished, advanced meditator were able to describe the experience, this would not be the exact experience of anyone else. Also, there would occur the very common error of followers taking the written word as some sort of concrete fact or instruction—even as a commandment. In this case, all the previous advice given by the Buddha would be wasted. The only way to understand an experience is to experience it. Try it for yourself.

Another's description, no matter how clear it reads in print, is that particular writer's experience. Even if that writer were a saint, what they experienced still could not be communicated to another person. A meditation teacher may offer only guidelines, put up signposts, draw maps. The most accomplished master can do no more. The recipe is not the cake and the instruction is not the experience, nor the map the treasure chest.

All of this lies, in part, behind the reason for saying: 'Who speaks knows not; who knows speaks not.' No secrets, only the near impossibility of putting a personal experience into comprehensible words. Hoping for someone, even the Buddha, to hand us enlightenment on a plate shows how far we still have to go.

6

GOD AND THE SOUL IN BUDDHIST PHILOSOPHY AND RELIGION

✣

There is probably more mistranslation and misunderstanding regarding the Buddha's teachings on the subject of 'self' and the 'soul' than the rest of the teachings put together. As these mistakes were made by early followers, they have persisted and been repeated by those coming later. The causes of the mistakes have been lack of proficiency in the translation of Pali and Sanskrit texts, carelessness, or an incompatible philosophic background. Not being a Pali or Sanskrit scholar myself, I have relied, in this book, mainly on translators proficient in the Pali, Sanskrit and English languages and on the most recently available translations into English of the early and later sutras.

The assumption of a creator God, first cause, is alien to the Buddhist philosophy of 'becoming', which is: no beginning, no end, but eternal change, dependent origination and impermanence. Whatever occurs does so because of innumerable causes. If one grain of sand on a beach is moved, this affects the whole beach and ultimately the universe. Nothing comes from nothing.

Misunderstanding this doctrine fills the non-Buddhist hearer with the fear that if impermanence is true then annihilation of the self must follow bodily death. Oblivion! Nothing! Out like an extinguished candle! Such fear is understandable for a person without the correct view of the anatta texts, the doctrine of 'no-soul'.

WHAT IS THE SOUL?

The soul is said by most theologically minded people to be an entity apart from the physical body, eternal and not subject to change. It is given by God and taken back to God at the moment of death or shortly after. The soul is sometimes spoken of as the breath of God—it is breathed into the body at birth and withdrawn at death. The 'soul' is also spoken of as being the seat of the emotions, as when someone says they were 'stirred to the depths of their soul'. The soul is seen as pure and the body as a foul hindrance to holiness—the body must be subdued in order to 'liberate' the soul, which is seen as a prisoner in a carnal prison. This is the premise behind excessive asceticism in many religious people, and sometimes behind—subconsciously—the active seeking of martyrdom by the fanatic.

Although the soul is said to be pure and permanent, there is also existing in conjunction with that belief the opposite belief that the soul can be corrupted by the impure body (which appears to be separate from the mind). Hence the belief in salvation and damnation—the soul can be 'saved' or it can be consigned to everlasting torment, even though it is the gift, or breath, of God.

Ancient religions are full of fascinating stories about the souls of the dead. Because of the wealth of colourful records preserved in tombs, in myth and in folklore and legends, we know that the idea of a soul—a spirit or a shade—existing after bodily death is a very old and wide-spread idea. The soul comes to be seen as the individual, the person. Taken further, the soul becomes the real 'I', an unchangeable core of personal being. And here lies the difference between the theological philosophy of existence and Buddhist philosophy, which teaches that there is no eternally unchangeable, concrete 'entity' as that which, in theological terms, is the 'soul'.

When a person is told there is no such thing as an 'I', what they hear is a statement that *they* do not exist, that there is no identity called John or Anne or Mum or Mr Prime Minister or whoever; that what they see before them in the mirror does not exist. Without further investigation they cannot be blamed for thinking their informant is fit to be locked away in a quiet asylum. There are thousands of people who consider themselves Buddhists who do not understand this teaching and do not *want* to understand it. Many are incapable of grasping its importance to the proper understanding of what the Buddha really taught.

If something does not exist it is not necessary or possible to negate it. What Buddhism teaches is *not* the need to get rid of the 'I', but to understand the non-existence of such a phenomenon. For centuries before and after the time of the Buddha, right to this present moment, there are and have been people doing violence in the form of excessive ascetic practices to their body and mind, in a desperate effort to negate the 'I'. All unnecessary and sadly misleading. There is no 'I'.

A lifetime spent naked on a mountain peak, or in an isolated cave existing on weeds or the charity of those who see the hermit as holy, or a lifetime spent in self-denying good works, may bring wonderful insights. It may even lead to full enlightenment, but it won't get rid of the 'I'.

What is this 'I' that so many earnest seekers after truth try hard to cut out of themselves? What is this 'I' which seems our most precious possession? For many non-Buddhists the 'I' is regarded as the soul—the *real* self. Whole libraries of philosophical works have been and will continue to be written about the 'I', so important is the idea to us. And therein lies the answer to the question of what is the 'I'.

The 'I' is an idea. The 'I' is merely a label. The 'I' does not exist any more than the label on a jam jar is jam itself. The jam can be said to 'exist' in that we can see it, touch it, taste it and smell it, but the jam is not the same as the label 'jam'.

'I' is a label we place on a collection of aggregates—matter, sensations, perceptions, mental formations, consciousness—and these factors themselves are constantly changing. They are impermanent, so just what are we labelling? What is 'me' at any given moment?

This 'I' to which we cling so desperately as being eternally unchanging is an impossibility, but the *idea* has its use as a label for the phenomenon, the 'person'. There *is* therefore an 'I' or self, but it is only a label for use in conventional truth, which is the truth within which we function in the world. Ultimate truth shows us the non-existence of any solid, concrete, inherently existing phenomenon. We are so accustomed to acting and reacting with labels that we seldom investigate what the label is really attempting to describe. We use a form of mental-verbal shorthand most of the time. It facilitates everyday human communication. But it is often simply borrowed without considering its truth or error, or whether, in actual fact, it is what we, as individuals, really think if we bother to think about it at all.

Buddhism teaches that existence is in a constant state of flux. Nothing remains the same for the time taken to blink an eye. A little serious investigation will show this to be so. And nothing exists *inherently*, in isolation, created by itself. Whatever 'is' at any moment depends on everything else that 'is' at that moment and ever was anywhere. When we move a grain of sand, when a leaf falls, when we breathe, even when we think—we have made a change in the universe. We are mistaken in our *idea* of the 'soul', the 'self', the 'I'. Whatever we might *think* it is, it too is subject to change—it is a compound phenomenon.

There is no God almighty, creator, first cause, in Buddhism. In any case, the meaning of the word 'God' is as varied as the personal perceptions of it. We each imagine God according to what we need, what we are taught or what we have experienced. The creative God can be seen as a kind of father, a royal universal ruler, a vengeful despot, as immovable fate, sometimes a saviour, sometimes a destroyer—whatever society needs at a particular time.

The supreme god of the Buddha's time was Brahma. His priests were the holders of all knowledge about him. They were, because of this knowledge, the mediators between the gods and humanity. Only they could offer the sacrifices donated by the people and only they could interpret the divine instructions. They were a caste, and to be a Brahmin one had to be born into that caste. Brahma—the Atman—was in many respects similar to the Jewish–Christian–Islamic concept of almighty God.

It was not the Buddha's custom to personally contradict the beliefs of those who came to question him. His method of teaching was to encourage the questioner to do their own investigative thinking. He used folktales and parables, metaphors and examples that would be intelligible to a particular person or audience.

The idea of a personal soul (ātman in Sanskrit) was the main religious belief of the Buddha's time, but not of his teaching. It is the ātman that is reincarnated again and again, in different life forms and different circumstances until it is so purified that it returns to, is united with, the creator, the Atman. This personal ātman is considered to be the thinker of one's thoughts, the feeler of one's sensations and the receiver of rewards and punishments for one's good or evil deeds. The idea of the ātman is the idea of self: 'I' think, therefore 'I' am. The desire of every believer in the Brahmanic religion was/is to be, at last, united with the Atman—united with God.

For persons believing in the soul (ātman) it would be pointless and confusing to simply state there is no ātman, unless it was possible for those persons to understand the explanation of that statement. There are several instances in Buddhist texts where the Buddha did not answer certain questions—not because he did not know the answer but because the enquirer was not, at that time, able to understand what was being taught. A wanderer named Vacchagotta came to the Buddha again and again with questions showing clearly his lack of intellectual understanding of the Dharma. Buddha did not reply and Vacchagotta went away to puzzle over both his question and the Buddha's silence. Eventually Vacchagotta came to fully understand, and so became an arahant (an enlightened follower). This is an example of the Buddha's compassionate patience with those who were not quick to grasp his meaning.

Taking the mind to be 'self' is no better than taking the body to be the self. The mind or consciousness is subject to even more rapid change than the ever-changing body. Every moment of thought is change, is impermanent.

To intellectually understand the teaching of anatta (no-soul, no-self) is not difficult once one understands the teaching of anicca (impermanence). What is extremely difficult for most is to realise it—to finally lose the feeling 'I am'.

The teaching of no-self is not to be thought of as 'I have no self'. This is the annihilationist theory and it is as incorrect as the thought 'I have self', which is the eternalist theory. The skilful way to *understand* the teaching is to hold neither opinion but to objectively investigate the matter for oneself, to resist the tendency to see Buddhism as teaching annihilation. Annihilation would be in direct contradiction to the teaching of anicca (impermanence). The teaching is not of an 'end' but of *constant change*: after this or that moment comes another moment, but a *different* moment. It gives a wonderful sense of continual adventure. Even the Buddhist symbol of a wheel, the circle of existence, is too static a symbol for the Dharma. It can

give the impression of the same round happening over and
over again. It does not emphasise the impossibility of
immutability. Nothing 'begins' or 'ends'. All phenomena
arise from conditions. Living as we do in a seemingly solid
world, this fluidity is difficult to experience. Investigation
and meditation will make it 'real', rather than of merely
academic interest—although a combination of both has a
great deal to be said for it.

WHO IS THE RELIGIOUS BUDDHA?

That question is really a contradiction in terms. The
Buddha did not teach religion. The Buddha did not
profess to be God, or a god, or the prophet of a god. He
did not profess to have received enlightenment from gods
or the messengers (angels) of a god. He did not offer
'salvation' to those who chose to listen to him, nor 'damnation' to those who did not, or could not. He dealt only
with reality and humanity as it is.

In the *Sabba Sutta Samyutta Nikaya* there is a passage
on metaphysics. The Buddha says:

Monks, I will teach you everything. Listen to it. What,
monks, is 'everything'? Eye and material form, ear and
sound, nose and odour, tongue and taste, body and tan-
gible objects, mind and mental objects. These are called
'everything'. A person might say, 'I will reject this "everything" and proclaim another "everything"'; he may certainly have a theory (of his own). But when questioned,
he would not be able to answer and would, moreover,
be subject to vexation. Why? Because it would not be
within the range of experience (avisaya).

For the Buddha, all else was speculation, fruitless for those still lost to hatred, greed and ignorance. If those who believed that countless reincarnations were necessary for the development of enlightenment spent time in idle speculation they would be wasting precious time. For those who sought enlightenment in this life, time was even more precious.

After the Buddha's death and the growth of large monasteries and Buddhist universities, philosophical speculation led to an immense diversity of teachings, coalescing into various sects, many verging closely on the religious. For the ordinary people, religion was easier to grasp than philosophy and they interpreted what they heard in ways acceptable to their minds and past beliefs, be they Vedic, Brahmin, Jain or amalgams of some or all of these.

Today, many Buddhists accept the Buddha as a 'saviour' and pray to him (as a Christian would to Jesus, a Hindu to the Hindu gods, a Muslim to Allah or, in some cases, the prophets).

As time went on there developed, from philosophical speculation, the bodhisattva ideal held by the Mahayana sects. The bodhisattva is the saint who, standing on the verge of enlightenment, foregoes 'entry into Nirvana' until they have helped every other sentient being to full enlightenment. From this comes the acceptance of nirvana as a *place*, the subsequent belief in the 'heavenly' pure lands of the bodhisattvas and the 'saving' granted by chanting the bodhisattva's name. Carried even further, it is the belief that speaking the bodhisattva's name once at the point of death will, by their grace, wipe out all adverse Karma and admit one to the saints' Pure Land. These beliefs offer great comfort to millions of people in

Buddhist countries. Time changes all things as people search for what suits their psychological makeup, or accept what previous generations have taught as truth.

The great sixth Patriarch of Chinese Buddhism, Hui Neng (AD638–713) had this to say regarding the Pure Land doctrine:

The Pure Lands are 84,000 miles away.
Therefore clear your minds and you are there.

In Buddhist speech, 84,000 miles represents many defilements, or non-skilful attitudes of mind and habitual non-virtuous behaviour.

The belief in the 'saving' grace of a bodhisattva's name and a Pure Land stems from misunderstandings of the meaning of the words 'samsara' and 'nirvana'—samsara as the world and its sufferings, and nirvana as somewhere else. The correct meaning of samsara is the not yet enlightened state and nirvana means the enlightened state.

Any attempt to discover, or more correctly to *re*cover the Buddha's teachings requires the understanding that even before the Dharma left India it had already absorbed, through its followers, much belief that was early Hindu, Rigvedic, Atharavedic and from the Brahmanas. Not everyone who followed the Buddha understood what he taught. Many interpreted the teachings through their previously held ideas. Some of the very early non-Buddhist inclusions were:

Posthumous reward and punishment, Karma with a
    capital K.
Hell, a place of endless darkness.

Sacrifice to gods.

Cosmology (Brahman).

Gifts to priests.

Belief in gods.

The belief in the accumulation of 'merit' to offset the
effects of 'bad' Karma in future lives.

The amount of so-called 'Buddhist' teachings from earlier
Indian belief systems incorporated after the death of
Buddha Sakyamuni is quite staggering.

The Buddha's rival teacher in his own time was the
Jain, Mahavira. Some Jains converted to Buddhism,
finding it a more 'comfortable' philosophy and way of
life. The Buddha's Middle Way was a far cry from the
extreme asceticism of the 'sky-clad' (that is, naked) ones.
Jain belief did not accept women as capable of 'ultimate
release', therefore Jain women, no matter how hard they
studied or practised, never reached the state of stark
nakedness that marked a Jain yogi. Converts, many long-
and well-versed in their own religious tenets, were of a
particular mindset and therefore interpreted the Buddha's
teachings accordingly, as did Brahmin and converts from
other belief systems.

It seems the Buddha knew what he was about in not
putting his ideas into writing. The written word is as
much open to misunderstanding as the spoken word.

Tibet is an example of the above in respect of infiltra-
tion of extraneous matter into the Dharma. In their early
zeal, the first converts in Tibet bought, for gold, every
text offered as the words of the Buddha or of his disciples. Not all manuscripts were Buddhist, but who could
tell? How could anyone then have known which was
baby and which was bathwater, and who would have

risked discarding either? The result is one of the richest and most colourful of the Mahayana religious sects.

As the Dharma was introduced into other countries, it was always influenced by the previous religion and culture of those countries. It is notable that for all the accretions, the basic tenets have remained unchanged. Therefore it helps, when attempting to understand Buddhism, to view it through the culture in which it is found. This, of course, applies to any of the 'world' religions: Buddhism, Judaism, Christianity, Islam, animism and so on.

BUDDHIST TEACHINGS ABOUT DEATH

What is the meaning of the word 'death' for the non-Buddhist? The most common reply would probably be 'Death is the end'. Another reply might be 'Death is release from suffering'. Still another would certainly be 'Death is the last parting from loved ones', or 'The loss of a loved one', or even the prelude to experiencing heaven or hell, reward or punishment. Some might view another's death as the removal of a fetter that has bound the survivor. Yet others could view death as the loss of any reason for the survivor to go on.

For those whose religions teach that death will unite the soul with its creator in eternal bliss, there is a strong reluctance to put the belief to the test. Fortunately for the human race, most religious dogmas carry a clause forbidding precipitous entry into eternity before one has been formally invited.

It has been commonly accepted, because the Buddha never gave answers to questions of this nature, that he taught there is *nothing* after what we call death. This is not correct. What he did was discourage idle speculation on this or any such subject. To those who did speculate he simply asked if anyone had returned to give them provable information. What he *did* have to say on the subject is explained in the anicca doctrine—impermanence, constant change, flux—and those teachings apply to what we call 'death' as well as to all else.

The subject of death is of great importance in Mahayana Buddhism, especially in the Tibetan sects. If we study Tibetan history, this preoccupation becomes more understandable. The old Bon religion (often referred to as a Demon religion) was based largely upon preparation for death and how to get safely through the Bardo to a fortunate rebirth. The Bardo is the passage through which the deceased's 'consciousness' passes, beset by disturbing sights and sounds, many terrifying, many strangely enticing, if not fully understood and expected. This passage lasts for *up to* forty-nine days. The type of passage experienced by the deceased will be in accordance with the preparation and understanding of what seems to be going on. The officiant, using *The Tibetan Book of the Dead*, 'speaks' with the deceased regarding what is happening, constantly reminding them to 'Be not afraid', because what seems to be happening is only a product of the mind. The officiant advises the deceased that they can come to no harm if the mind is kept firmly on the clear light which appears ahead and if it refuses to be distracted.

When Buddhism was accepted in Tibet in the seventh century AD, much of Bon was incorporated into it as many Bon monks converted. Today, one can find in Tibetan Buddhism much of what is still called the 'Old' eligion, practised inside and outside of Tibetan Buddhism. The present Chinese regime, in forcing so many learned monks to flee Tibet, may, in the long run, have saved for future study a most colourful branch of Mahayana Buddhism. That regime also forced His Holiness Tenzin Gyatso, the fourteenth incarnation of the Dalai Lama and head of the Gelugpa sect, whose work for peace on earth has been equalled by few others, to have personal contact with the West. Had he remained under Chinese dominance he may never have travelled outside Tibet and may never have made the contacts that are possible with modern, global communication technology.

Another gain for all people was the quantity or sacred texts the various lamas and monks were able to bring with them. Tibet had long been a treasure house of texts, many not yet translated into Western languages, while many more were destroyed with the monasteries, temples and monastic communities.

Death for most Buddhists of whatever sect or culture is usually seen as simply the prelude to *rebirth* into this world as a sentient being of whatever kind one's Karma dictates. Reincarnation is usually considered to lead to further human experience.

This entire subject is of the utmost importance to *religious* Buddhists and many live their lives in such a way to gain 'merit' towards a fortunate rebirth. It is believed merit can be gained by such methods as participation in rituals, by chanting literally millions of mantras, by building stupas, by prostrating oneself to the point of exhaustion, by vows of silence, by fasting, by pilgrimages, by making offerings (in fact in all very much the same ways as the members of any religion attempt to purchase their way into whatever is their idea of a happy next life here

or in 'heaven'). Sometimes the methods used to gain
merit may seem superstitious or primitive to a non-
Buddhist, having developed from cultures much older
than Buddhism, but the practices make a Buddhist population the least contentious, least criminally inclined
amongst human beings.

Here is an interesting excerpt to illustrate the above. It
is taken from the Roman Catholic newspaper, *The Tablet*,
and quotes from the British census of 1881 in India,
regarding crime:

Convictions:	Europeans	1 in 274 of pop.
	Eurasians	1 in 509 "
	Native Christians	1 in 799 "
	Mahommedans	1 in 856 "
	Hindus	1 in 1361 "
	Buddhists	1 in 3787 "

[The English writer's comment was:] It appears from these
figures that while we effect a very marked moral deteriora-
tion in the natives by converting them to our creed, their
natural standard of morality is so high that, however much
we Christianise them, we cannot altogether succeed in
making them as bad as ourselves.

What is the connection between gaining merit, and so
on, with the Buddhist attitude to death? It is that the Buddhist is fully aware that no-one knows the hour or
manner of their death and that the next rebirth/reincar-
nation will be the balancing out of the good and bad
Karma of their actions in *this* human life. It behoves them
to create as little bad Karma as possible and to create as
much good Karma (merit) as possible while the opportunity to do so presents itself.

Death is a most suitable subject for meditation. Buddhists do not fear death, accepting its inevitability as part of the birth/death cycle. For a Buddhist, death cannot be the 'end'. What we call death cannot be a 'concrete', everlasting, unchanging event. It can be only the end of a phase, or a stage in becoming 'something else'. We do not even know what death is, when it occurs, at what exact point it is complete. When I was a young nurse it was the custom, once death was 'confirmed' by a medical practitioner, to straighten the body, tie up the jaw and leave further attention (laying-out) for one hour. Just to make sure? Or instinctive 'knowledge'?

There are no 'ends' in Buddhism. Ends imply beginnings. Ends and beginnings have no relevance to the Buddha's teachings. He taught impermanence, flux, constant change, dependent origination. Even the ultimate gaining of nirvana (enlightenment) is not an end but, as he said, 'No more of this state', a never-ending becoming, whatever that becoming may turn out to be. The idea of the beginning or end of a life-stream is impossible for a Buddhist to accept. According to the Buddha's words,

> . . . this cycle of continuity [samsara—unenlightenment] is without a visible end, and the first beginnings of beings wandering and running around, enveloped in ignorance and bound down by the fetters of thirst [desire, tanhā] is not to be perceived.
>
> The first beginning of ignorance [avijja] is not to be perceived in such a way as to postulate that there was no ignorance beyond a certain point.

The word 'ignorance' in Buddhist teachings does not mean lack of knowledge or education or intelligence but simply lack of the inner wisdom that is the potential for full enlightenment. So in Buddism it is not possible to say that what we call 'life' begins or ends. To fear *inescapable* change makes no sense to a Buddhist. Therefore there is no need for despair regarding the subject of eventual physical death—one's own or that of others. Nothing lasts forever—neither happiness nor unhappiness. Enjoy the now and accept that it will change.

Non-Buddhists mistakenly see the Dharma as something solemn and cheerless, a sad acceptance of an inevitable existence of unremitting suffering, with the concept of Karma as supernatural punishment or reward, forever pressing down on all like a dark, heavy cloud. Buddhists would not recognise their religion in such a description. Buddhism does not ignore the suffering and grief caused by impending death or the recent loss of a loved one. One of the finest Buddhist parables is that of the young mother whose infant had died. She carried the body about, begging for help until the villagers sent her to the new, wonderful teacher who was then in the area in the hope that he might cure her madness. She came to the Buddha who saw clearly the level of her understanding and promised to help if she would leave the body with the sangha and go into the nearby town. He told her to find a mustard seed from a dwelling in which no-one had lost a loved one to death. She went with high hopes but at last returned with open, empty hands, having learned that no-one escapes the sorrow of losing a loved one. She allowed the cremation of her child's body and requested to become one of the Buddha's followers. The Buddha discovered the way *out* of suffering and it is there for anyone to learn if they are mentally and spiritually inclined to do so. Words won't teach this, practice will.

Buddhists are not generally given to revering the bodily remains of the deceased except in the matter of relics of sages and saints. To establish large cemeteries filled with monuments made to endure as long as possible does not make sense to them. There stands the expensive grave statuary and mausoleum but 'no-one' is there. Loved ones are not, as one often hears non-Buddhists say, 'in the grave'. The religious Buddhist, of whatever sect, believes that loved ones and all the ancestors are more than the body only. They have 'passed on' to a further state. According to some sects, they will return, reincarnated, to work out their Karma.

It is useful at this stage to contemplate what it is that goes onward in the continuity of becoming. Buddha taught that it is the thirst of the life force, the desire (tanhā) for continual becoming—another birth which, of course, will lead to another death and so on. Tanhā ceases through pānnā (wisdom). This pānnā is within oursleves and can be developed in this life. With the advent of pānnā the continual round is overcome so that future 'change' can proceed in a different 'direction'. The hope of a happy reincarnation is one way of putting the chance of enlightenment in *this* life into the 'too hard' basket. Plenty of time in future life! We are a mentally lazy lot. Not unintelligent, just lazy. We would rather put up with the mess of our lives than set to work to clean it up so as to be able to really enjoy what we have now, which, of course, has already ceased to exist.

There is an interesting reply given by one of Buddha's disciples to the question, 'Does a man live after death?' The reply was as follows: 'We do not know whether he is the body, or in the body, or other than the body whilst alive. How can we know whether, after the death of the body, he is dead?' *Dhātuvibanga-sutra* (No 140), Majjhima-nikaya.

Despite all the philosophical discussion regarding the subject of death, religious Buddhism does not deny its followers any of the rituals and ceremonies that may be of help to the bereaved. Sangha members do carry out these rituals. They also offer compassionate 'counselling' if asked and continue this for as long as the bereaved require.

DEATH AND DYING

Amongst Western Buddhists of the Tibetan tradition in this country, a hospice movement is growing. It is quite undenominational—voluntary, free, palliative care such as is offered by various secular and religious groups in the community. The idea behind all such services is to give the terminally ill the chance to end their lives in their own, familiar, home environment. This often gives a sufferer the peace, quiet and lack of unnecessary intervention that permits, if needed, the chance to accept and perhaps understand better what is happening. Pain relief with strict attention to the dignity of the individual is the mainstay of the service. Nursing and medical care is given by professionals.

Although being a practising Buddhist, religious or philosophical, may seem at first glance to be living a life in preparation for death (without time to live life itself), this is an utterly mistaken concept. Because Buddhists have, without reserve, faced the simple fact of the inevitability of physical death and accepted this as a natural part of life, they are then free to make the most of every moment as it comes, without anxiety as to the moment to follow—whether or not there should be a following moment. Such freedom! This is not to say that one can face the death of loved ones without pain. What it does do is allow the soon-to-be-bereaved to let the dying go without adding to that suffering by distressful shows of their inability to carry on without them. Compassion means understanding the suffering of others without exhibiting one's own. Grief is a natural phenomenon for which Buddhist practice seeks to prepare us, so that we suffer a less disruptive grief, not necessarily a less heartfelt grief.

It is mere speculation as to whether or not what we call the 'identity' of the person continues after what we call death. Perhaps it is that whatever is 'real' about us continues, in some way, developing along lines we cannot now imagine. For those who are concerned with thoughts of some kind of continuity, my discussion offers food for thought but not for the formulating of beliefs and 'certainties'. All else is imaginary speculation and not conducive to the development of wisdom or knowledge.

In the texts there is a phrase often used by the Buddha regarding the accomplishment of 'release' from samsara (the condition of ignorance). This phrase speaks of the fully awakened and it says 'what has to be done is done, there is no more to be done *on this account*'. The last words in the phrase are often translated as 'in this state'. Whichever translation is used it is clear that there is no 'end', even for the fully enlightened arahat.

It can be seen that whether the Buddhist chooses to accept belief in reincarnation complete with personal memories, or simple rebirth in another form without personal identity, or the further becoming of whatever reality lies in the sentient being, there is no 'end'. No eternal annihilation of being. No *event* goes on forever. One is not *forever* being born or *forever* dying. One is not *forever* a child, *forever* a mature adult or *forever* an aged person. Even within each of those phases one is constantly changing. Only change, impermanence, continues.

Part of the *Sabbasava Sutra* is a list of subjects the Buddha taught as only speculation:

1. Did I exist in the past?
2. Did I not exist in the past?
3. What was I in the past?
4. How was I in the past?
5. Having been what, did I become what in the past?
6. Shall I exist in the future?
7. Shall I not exist in the future?
8. What shall I be in the future?
9. How shall I be in the future?
10. Having been what, shall I become what in the future?

Or now, at the present time he is doubtful about himself:

11. Am I?
12. Am I not?
13. What am I?
14. How am I?
15. Whence came this person?
16. Whither will he go?

When he reflects unwisely in this way, one of the six false views arises in him:

1. I have a Self: this view arises in him as true and real.
2. I have no Self: this view arises in him as true and real.
3. By Self I perceive Self: this view arises in him as true and real.

4. By Self I perceive non-Self: this view arises in him as true and real.

5. By non-Self I perceive Self: this view arises in him as true and real.

6. Or a wrong view arises in him as follows: This is my Self, which speaks and feels, which experiences the fruits (outcomes) of good and bad actions now here and now there. This Self is permanent, stable, everlasting, unchanging, remaining the same for ever and ever.

(extract from the *Satta* quoted in Walpola Rahula, *What the Buddha Taught*).

This was another instance of the Buddha's advice to his hearers not to waste precious time trying to solve the unsolvable and that insight leading to full enlightenment brings with it wisdom or knowledge. All things are clear to the fully enlightened mind.

What quantum science would say is that what continues after physical dissolution can only be ever-changing patterns of probability, particle activity that cannot be predicted. In other words, *anything* could happen. Trying to predict the unpredictable is not conducive to gaining real knowledge but is sidetracking the mind from important matters. Here science and Buddha Sakyamuni are in full agreement, as in so many other instances.

THE AFTERLIFE

The human need for a supernatural father/mother figure/s is involved intrinsically with the psychological makeup of an individual and would appear to be as old as the present state of the human mind. Every person has a slightly different psychological makeup even though categories can be used in the formulation of theories. A person's psychological makeup is determined by genetic inheritance plus everything that happens in that person's sphere of experience during early development and/or later.

The person who has enjoyed a perfectly satisfactory, well-balanced nurturing in infancy and childhood may, if religiously minded, have the expectation of such an experience in what is seen as the next life. To expect otherwise would negate the whole anthropomorphic idea of God the father/mother on which so much religion is based. (In Catholicism, the mother of Jesus supplies the maternal aspect.)

For those whose infancy has been without full parental nurturing, be it lack of mothering or lack of the presence of the father, the expectation could well be of a god anthropomorphised as completely mother or completely father.

In a strongly patriarchal culture, the expectation of God would naturally be of an authoritarian male figure, the all-knowing he-who-must-be-obeyed on pain of dis-inheritance or death.

In a religious matriarchal culture, God may be the life-giver, the dispenser of non-discriminating love, even the teacher (as is the human mother at her best), as well as the wrathful destroyer of her children's enemies.

Religious Buddhism, in particular the Mahayana and Vajrayana (Tantrism), brings together what has become divided—mother / father, male / female—the yin / yang principle. It is based on neither the fully and exclusively male principle nor the fully exclusively female principle, but transcends both, following always and in all things the Middle Path—becoming not one nor the other, but 'both', in a complete whole.

In religious Buddhism, although Siddhartha Gautama was indeed of the male sex, in religius practice he is not seen as a male figure at all, but in a non-sexual aspect of full enlightenment or Buddhahood. This makes unnecessary the addition of a female god in the form of the ever-virgin or spouse. Yasodarah, his wife, has not been elevated to sainthood or spiritual consort, because tl was not compatible with the philosophy out of which religion developed.

❧

7

SOME QUESTIONS
AND SOME ANSWERS

*(with which it is hoped no-one will
wholly agree)*

❧

It is good to question, especially in matters of religion,
where one is often expected by the instructor to
accept what is imparted purely on faith. Questioning is
not necessarily the same as doubting. To question is to
seek further information. One may wish strongly to
believe what is spoken or written yet be unable to do so
out of blind faith only.

Questioning is not always a sign of not knowing but
often simply a desire for clarification if the source of
information seems obscure; yet, in religion, the questioner is often made to feel guilty of a crime against not

only the instructor but against the very deity itself.

The competent Buddhist teacher respects those who question as serious seekers-after-wisdom/knowledge. Questions are indications of the seeker's level of understanding of the dharma. The questions asked are also an indication of the level of the questioner's present knowledge and philosophical outlook on life.

In religious matters there is much talk of belief and unbelief, believers and unbelievers. We are proud of the strength with which we cling to our beliefs, but to be able to *believe* something it is surely necessary to understand it. I can *believe* that flour and eggs and butter and sugar mixed together and baked will result in a cake because (a) I have seen it done many times or (b) I can do it myself—actually *experience* it. I can believe that the venom of certain insects and reptiles may kill; that sharp points and blades may cause injury; that lack of rain may ruin my farm; that not only cats but some birds eat birds. I can *believe* all these things and hundreds of thousands more for the same reasons. Believing in something I know nothing about and cannot investigate is pointless indeed, and manifestly incorrect semantics according to Buddhist teachings.

The most unfortunate outcome of a 'belief' based on faith only is that it is so final; it precludes the believer's advance in knowledge of the subject; it is, in fact, a brick wall blocking further experience. It is also an easy, self-satisfying escape route from further mental engagement and helps the believer to feel strong and 'saved' with a 'rock' to cling to.

To question is to learn, even if the answers are not necessarily always correct, provided the questioner goes on to question the answers. It is not always comfortable to be a questioner living in a community of believers who may often judge the 'unbeliever' to be a blasphemous heretic, but questioning is well worth it in the long run. The final resolution of such an uncomfortable situation is to leave the community, rather than remain while appearing to demean the beliefs of others. This solution will remove distraction for both 'sides' and is my personal reason for spending more time in the lay community than in large communities of Sangha members.

An attempt will be made here to answer some of the questions most commonly asked by non-Buddhists regarding what they may have read or observed or been told of Buddhist practices and doctrines. At the same time it is fervently hoped that questioners will not believe the answers but will insist on investigating until they can experience for themselves the truth or otherwise of those answers. Written answers can never be as satisfactory as answers given orally in a one-to-one situation, where assessment can be made of the level of understanding of the questioner. A facial expression of perplexity, a glazing of the eye, a sigh or slight shake of the head—any of these can alert the teacher that they are not putting the information clearly enough for this individual seeker. The written word can often veil what the writer really means, especially when attempting to put profound thoughts into simple words.

Q: *Why did the Buddha bother to teach when there was already in place at least one religion with all the authority of an upper class in charge of it?*

A: From the teachings it becomes apparent that the Brahmin and Jain religions had become extremely ritualised, the Brahmin filled with superstition and

based largely on animal sacrifice, without the animal
itself being considered in any way sacred. The important part of the sacrifice was blood. The poor, who
were in most need of blessings, became even poorer
as they attempted to gain blessings by giving the
Brahmin priests animals and birds to offer to the
myriad deities. The deeper philosophy behind the
origins of the religion was being lost.

The were many who, like the Buddha, once family
duty was done, left the comforts of domesticity and
wandered about seeking to understand why there was
so much ignorance, greed, lack of lasting satisfaction
and suffering in life. It was a time when many believed
physical deprivation and painful suffering would free
the mind for greater understanding. Others believed in
over-indulgence; some worshipped fire, and others
eschewed even clothing for their bodies and ingested
only water and one particular type of herb or weed.
These practices often produced deep trances and hallucinations. These were regarded as great attainments,
and hallucinations brought about by starvation were
considered revelations.

For seven years, Siddhartha Gautama tried all the
methods recommended by acknowledged sages and
found no satisfactory answers in them. There had to
be another way—a middle way, as it turned out.

The main trigger for the Buddha's quest was compassion—compassion for suffering sentient beings,
not just for himself. He did not set out to found a
religion or establish monasteries—those things were
merely natural progressions as more and more people
came to follow him and to attempt to grasp what he
taught. The Buddha taught for more than half his life

but it will not necessarily take that long for a persevering seeker to learn what he taught. For us it is
questioning, not faith, that is needed for proper comprehension of the teachings of the Enlightened One,
the Sage of the Sakya clan, Buddha Sakyamuni, Sage
of the World. He did not set out to undermine the
prevailing religions, but when someone came to
discuss their beliefs with him he did his best to stimulate the speaker to deeper thought.

Q: *Are there Buddhist teachings regarding heaven and
   hell?*

A: No, there are not. The teachings are metaphors for
   states of mind experienced in this life.

Q: *Is the Dalai Lama the Buddhist 'Pope'?*

A: No. His Holiness the Dalai Lama is, as he often states,
   a simple Tibetan Buddhist monk, head of the
   Gelugpa sect. The special reverence paid to him by
   Tibetans is due to their belief in his being the reincarnation of Chenrezig, the Buddha of compassion, a
   Tibetan Buddhist concept stemming from the anthro-
   pomorphising of an abstract idea of the compassionate aspect of the Buddha nature.

Q: *Is the Mahayana school more 'Buddhist' than the
   Theravada?*

A: No. The basic tenets of both are Buddhist but each
   differs on some philosophical points that developed
   after the Buddha's death, or, as religious Buddhists
   say, his parinirvana, his 'entry' into nirvana.

Q: *Why must nuns take so many more vows than monks?*

A: The greater number of vows for nuns is often seen
   as anti-women but, although it would not be correct
   for me to go into detail on this point, unless to a
   woman seeking ordination, it is a fact that many of

the extra vows were for the protection of nuns when they were not living in the monasteries. Delightful as it would be if women (and men) could travel in safety at all times and not have their appearance or demeanour misinterpreted, this was not, and is not, the case *anywhere*. Buddhism deals with facts, not what 'ought to be'. Many such vows have been kept in the Vinaya although time has made them irrelevant. The right-minded act accordingly.

Q: *Do women have the opportunity to become leaders?*

A: Definitely, if that is their way. They may become gurus, teachers, or heads of monasteries, and are often considered holy by their followers and disciples.

Q: *Are monks considered to be 'higher' than nuns?*

A: In a monastery or at the time of the Rains Retreat this may appear to be so in some cases, but this is a matter for individuals. A learned monk or nun is respected, gender notwithstanding, while, on the other hand, even some monks and nuns carry a chip on their shoulder in this regard, as do some laypersons. Attitudes based on gender are cultural, not Buddhist.

Q: *Is it considered that only monastics may become enlightened?*

A: Definitely not. There are no such beliefs nor is such a belief taught in Buddhism. There have been, and one hopes will be, many scholarly, dedicated lay teachers demonstrating high attainments. Some have been monks or nuns, some have never contemplated the monastic life.

Q: *Why would someone brought up as a Christian (Catholic or non-Catholic) or a Jew, Hindu, Muslim or any other, turn to Buddhism for answers?*

A: Obviously, for the serious seeker-after-wisdom/
knowledge, the answer is that the religion in which
they were raised has failed to give satisfactory
answers. The cause of this lack of lasting satisfaction
is often the fault of those who see themselves as
knowledgeable teachers but who do not fully understand the tenets of their own religion and who discourage questions they cannot answer. This applies
very much to some of the so-called scripture 'teachers' in schools, where mostly legends and folkstories
are used as 'instruction'. For the intelligent, questing
mind, this often leads to confusion and outright
disbelief, and may stunt the desire for investigation.
Hearing and reading something of Buddhist philosophy, the seeker may decide to go on with the search.

Then there are the 'trippers' and the 'wine tasters'
(never more than a sip) and the devotional types of
people who need something to be the focus of their
devotion. The variety of people attracted to Buddhism from other religions are as diverse as there are
human psychological characteristics, some being
attracted more to the culture than to the religion.

Q: *Why do Buddhist monks and nuns shave their heads?*

A: In the days of the Buddha, as today, hair was a person's crowning glory. Much time could be spent
caring for it and dressing it becomingly with jewels
and flowers for personal satisfaction, and for the
purpose of attracting attention. As Sangha numbers
grew, this was found not to be in the interests of
serious study. Therefore it became the custom that on
ordination the 'crowning glory' was shorn—a sign of
renunciation of both vanity and the desire for admiration. When one lives under monastic conditions, a

shaven head arouses no interest, but if one lives outside the monastery, one does what is most appropriate in the circumstances. Being the only Buddhist I know of in the country town where I live, to be jeered at by some young people as a 'skinhead' (at the age of 72!) would seem to be calling down ridicule on this practice and perhaps therefore on Buddhism in the minds of those with little or no knowledge of it. (Therefore I do not shave my head.)

Q: *What is the Buddhist attitude to marriage?*

A: Much the same as that of Christianity, Judaism or Islam: marriage is a contract between a man and a woman to love, honour and cherish each other and the children of their union. Adultery is contrary to the Buddhist precept of no unlawful sexual activity. Divorce is a civil, not a religious, matter.

Q: *Isn't Buddhism a sexist, patriarchal religion?*

A: No. To a practising Buddhist, especially a religious one believing in reincarnation, men and women change places often in other lives so that one sees people just as people, no matter what sex they may be in this life. The philosophic Buddhist knows that, male or female, we are *all* suffering sentient beings— right now.

Q: *Don't Buddhists pray to be reborn as males so they can achieve enlightenment?*

A: No. 'Real' Buddhists do not. This idea is very much pre-Buddhist and a 'hangover' in some cultures, popular with those whom it flatters.

Q: *Must all Buddhist monks and nuns always wear their robes?*

A: Not when it is inappropriate. For those who live and work in a Western-style society, where there is no lay financial support, whatever is appropriate may be worn. The robes are always carried, though symbolised by blessed scraps of yellow cloth, when travelling in lay clothes. One has vowed not to be without one's robes, begging bowl and water strainer. These are constant reminders of one's ordination vows.

Q: *How can one know which is the most suitable sect to approach?*

A: My advice is to study as much as you can of them all. On the other hand, it does not really matter where you begin, as you will soon find *your* way if you continually investigate what you are told. My first interest was in Theravadin teachings but the nearest place of instruction was Tibetan so I began there. Now, many years later, I call myself simply a 'Buddha Buddhist' and am deeply thankful to *all* who have helped me find my way along the path.

Q: *Is it a fact that Buddhists should not be interested in increasing their possessions?*

A: No. At no time has Buddhism ever advocated voluntary poverty. It does teach what all people know—that wealth does not insulate us from dukha and that to exploit other sentient beings for gain is ethically reprehensible. Buddha in fact advised wealthy people and business people how to remain prosperous, but to give a fair day's pay for a fair day's work.

A PERSONAL NOTE

During question time, after I have given a talk on the Dharma, there is one question sure to be asked. It is why—not how—I, a Western woman of some wordly experience, was initially attracted to the teachings of the Buddha. Here is the best explanation I can give, being, like all humankind, no expert at seeing my own motives and reasons with fullest clarity.

My interest in ancient history, anthropology, archaeology, mythology, religion and mysticism (all nurtured by the books my father used to send me once I turned fourteen) resulted in a lack of satisfaction with the didactic tenets of the main religions—Hinduism, Judaism, Christianity and Islam. I am the type of person who dislikes being told what to do unless I understand, at least to some extent, what the expected result might be.

I was a very religious child, educated partly in Catholic schools and a regular attendant at the rituals of my religion. I was not deterred, even by maternal scorn and ridicule. I wanted so very much to *believe*, as others seemed able to do; to have such a sure faith with no nagging questions forever being asked by my questing mind. Ultimately, I attempted to find satisfactory answers in many Christian sects, and while I met many sincere, kindly people, those who professed to be teachers were of no help where my questions were concerned.

I read the Old and New Testaments many times over the years, but the Old Testament, in view of my early reading of ancient history and mythology, seemed too patently to be tribal interpretations of earlier history from other cultures. This undermined my ability to take it, and its offshoot—Christianity—on faith alone. At the same time I envied, and still do, those who have such strong faith, such ability to believe what they do not understand. This peace of mind was not for me. I did not realise then that what I was seeking was not so much a religion, but a philosophy to live by and which would make sense of existence.

Present-day Islam's ideas of paradise as instant reward for death in a jihad (or holy war), plus the Muslim attitude to women, I found distasteful, although I could admire the actual social teachings of the prophet Mohammed and found much of Sufism appealing.

Hinduism I found fascinating as a historical and philosophical study, but not as a religion for myself.

I was looking for answers that made sense of the general muddle that life seemed to me to be and nowhere but in the teachings, the basic early teachings, of the Buddha did I find a way to discover those answers.

There is no intention on my part to denigrate the beliefs held sacred by others of no matter what religion. I am attempting only as complete an answer to the original question as I am able. The impulse to religious belief, to my way of thinking, is an integral part of human nature, though it may take many forms. And if there should be a supreme intelligence, or a creator of all, then I fail to see why there should be so much animosity, even hatred, caused by the use of different names for that, for want of a better word, 'entity'. To me, these matters are for personal consideration, with those scholars of the subject being studied for their *opinions*. The final understanding will be a personal experience that cannot be forced on others or even branded as the truth.

Really, in the final analysis, words are not of much use in matters above and beyond language. We are a mentally lazy lot, not yet aware of how much mind/brain power we have and forever seeking salvation handed to us on a platter. Salvation from what? The only thing I felt we needed salvation from was our own ignorance, and that salvation comes with personal experience within as complete an awareness as can possibly be cultivated.

No-one, no ritual, no wish-without-effort, no divine grace can confer such salvation as a gift as might a magician in a fairytale. It must be a unique personal experience. Others, Buddha included, can only point the way.

This is what I was seeking. Have I found what I was seeking? Yes. Am I able to put it to proper use? I am practising (not 'trying') to do so, but there is no 'end' to this practising. Even enlightenment would not be an 'end', only another 'beginning'. The most valuable thing I have learned is to take personal responsibility for my actions and reactions as they influence present and future moments. If I mess it up I don't look for someone or something else to blame. I am always free to choose the direction of my next step and will have to accept the consequences. To me, this is a wonderful freedom and security—if there is any such thing. It doesn't make me any wiser as a person but it does mean that there is no-one I have finally to answer to but myself—and I want to live so the answering may be as easy as possible.

It is my sincere hope that all beings will eventually find all the questions and all the answers we, every one of us, seek to find.

May it be so

Reader, it is my hope that what you have read has raised many more questions than it has answered, leaving you with the desire to know more.

PUBLIC TALKS

Two lectures given to general audiences at the Melbourne Theosophical Society, 1996–97

๛

Namo Buddhaya

FREEDOM FROM GREED, HATRED AND IGNORANCE

My name is Adrienne Howley and before I begin this talk I wish to say how pleased I am to be here with people like yourselves who are willing to listen to differing views. While such willingness is a sign of human intelligence, open minds are far from common.

When I was first asked to speak here, I got out all my books and studied and scribbled and checked for accuracy and tried rigorously to keep myself out of it—until I was almost cross-eyed and had writer's cramp. Then at last the penny dropped. I did a spot of meditation and asked for help. I soon realised that if what I had done was what you wanted, then you may have—probably already have—done it for yourselves. So I tore it all up and tried to put into words what I have learned from my own personal experience of the Buddha's teachings and now, that is what I would like to share with you.

Tibetan Buddhist teachers offer a helpful suggestion before giving a Dharma talk. They call it the lesson of the three pots and I would like to offer it to you. This is how it goes: The first pot has a hole in it so that whatever goes in immediately leaks out. That pot can hold nothing. The second pot already contains so much material it cannot absorb any more. The third pot is clean and empty, ready to receive what is put into it. May I suggest we make our minds like the third pot for this talk? Let us close our eyes and listen to the tone of this ritual bell and as the tone fades away let our personal concerns go with it and for five minutes let our thoughts rise and pass away without attachment. I will ring the bell after that and we can bring our attention back with the fading tone.

Before I begin, let me tell you a little about my contacts with the Dharma. My initial contact happened more than thirty years ago when my elder son handed me a book titled *The Teachings of the Compassionate Buddha*. The contents grabbed my attention but there were no qualified teachers in Sydney at that time. There was a small Buddhist Society, but as a shiftworker I was seldom able to attend meetings. I could do little but read what came my way. I was far too busy making a mess of my life to do more than that.

Whenever life got to be a bit much I would joke that one day I would either live on top of Mount Everest or become a Buddhist nun. The joke became a self-fulfilling prophecy. I have been a nun for fourteen years in both the Tibetan tradition, in which nuns can only become novices, and the Vietnamese tradition, which holds the bhikkhuni lineage directly from ancient India through China.

I am not religious in the sense of relying on rites and rituals, and I avoid organised religion with its ready-made tenets and -isms because, for me, things of the 'spirit' are personal and a matter of continual learning. I do not tell you this in order to sound like a Buddhist expert. I can speak only of what I have learned from my own studies and investigations, and from the teachings I have received from those more learned than myself.

Buddhism is all about enlightenment and enlightenment means fully understanding or understanding as fully as our senses permit. Gautama Buddha taught from experience. He did not receive divine directions or messages from gods. He was a human being in full. He married and fathered children, as was the duty of his social position at the time. There was nothing mysterious about his life. He *was* extremely intelligent and earnest in his searching for a way for sentient beings to understand and overcome suffering—all kinds of suffering. He left his comfortable, princely life to study for more than six years with the greatest teachers of his place and time, even putting his life at risk in order to learn.

Having found, by his own efforts, the cause of suffering and the way out of it, he wondered if people would really want to know. Would they bother to listen? Compassion for all sentient beings caused him to begin teaching what he had learned.

For more than forty years he taught and gave advice to people from all walks of life, from kings or, as Indian people would say, maharajahs, to sudras—the untouchables. He taught according to the needs and capabilities of his hearers—something that is not always taken into consideration by would-be interpreters of the Dharma. Buddhism can be taught on many levels and with continuing study and practice becomes like a never-emptying treasure chest; one thinks one has extracted all that is in a given teaching, yet on returning to it one finds even greater treasures. It is a simple matter of persevering in the expansion of one's understanding and personal experience.

Buddha was no dogmatist. His constant injunction was that his hearers not believe what he said simply out of respect for him, but that they investigate matters for themselves. That is what a real Buddhist tries to do. What we learn is eventually a personal experience for each of us.

Freedom

According to Buddhist teachings, the entire human race in whatever age, in whatever country or culture, is and always has been seeking freedom. Freedom from what? Are we not all, right down to single-cell organisms, seeking freedom from suffering? And what do we mean by suffering? What Buddha called suffering, put into a few words, is dukha, which can be translated as pain/sorrow/misery. That was not quite what the Buddha meant. He had a wider view that included such ideas as 'imperfection', 'impermanence', 'insubstantiality'. There is

no *one* word to translate the whole concept. The traditional wording of the First Noble Truth says that dukha
is birth, old age, sickness, death, association with the
unpleasant and separation from the pleasant, not getting
what one desires, grief, lamentation, distress, and all the
forms of mental and physical sufferings of existence.

Buddha went into great detail to explain the cause of
all this suffering, because a problem cannot be corrected—except in the occasional hit-or-miss situation—
unless we find the cause. We can participate in all kinds
of distracting indulgences or all kinds of self-denial and
rituals, but these only alleviate our suffering momentarily,
just as an analgesic will momentarily alleviate a headache
but not cure whatever is causing it. One of our main
problems is that we prefer the analgesic to the hard work
and personal honesty required in order to discover the
cause of our suffering.

Before I go on I must, in fairness to Buddhist philosophy, point out that Buddha did not teach that *all* is
dukha. He did not deny the existence of beauty and the
possibility of joy. What he taught was that *this* is dukha—
our everyday existence. His aim in teaching was to show
us how to be happy right now and in the future from the
very next moment of *this* existence. The reason for dukha
(individual suffering, or lack of lasting satisfaction) can
be explained most easily under the three headings of
greed, hatred and ignorance, and it is under these headings that I am speaking today.

We need to have a clear idea of what is meant by
greed, by hatred and by ignorance, because at this
moment, each one of us knows, for sure, that we are not
greedy, we do not hate anyone enough to want to thump
them, and as for ignorance—how dare anyone cast such

a slur on us! We are educated, thinking beings! These three conditions might apply to others but certainly *not* to us! Now before anyone begins to feel insulted, let me explain what is meant here in the context of Buddhist teaching regarding these three words. Take the word that was originally translated as 'greed' or 'desire'. The clearer meaning of the Pali word would be desirousness, not simply desire, and it means that particular grasping kind of want/need with which we are born and without which nature would not permit us to survive. The first things we want/need in our innate desirousness are air, food and suitable ecological surroundings. Lucky us if these are found in the arms of a loving mother or parenting person, because we will then have, without effort, the next big need/want: love.

But all this is natural greed, natural desirousness and quite appropriate for infants who grasp at everything they can get their hands and mouths on. Everything they hold or behold is theirs (possessiveness) and they will throw some horrible tantrums when they are shown otherwise. We don't change much, do we? As adults we are still *inappropriately* possessive. This brings to my mind a bit of youthful wisdom from one of my sons. I was bemoaning, not for the first time, the fact that no matter what one did for or gave to my mother she was never satisfied. She would take it, of course, but left no doubt that it was the wrong colour or shape or not what she had really wanted. I said that she did not seem to know what she wanted. My son smiled and said quietly, 'Mother, you don't understand her. That's all. She *does* know what she wants—she just wants *everything*'. We are all a bit like that and some of us throw spectacular tantrums when we can't have it all, and suffer exceedingly and cause others to suffer also.

Even when we *do* get what we want, we will still suffer unless we have come to understand one of the Buddha's most important teachings: anicca—impermanence, change, constant flux. The newest, most costly car will deteriorate, the newest house will not remain forever new, our present love affair—the one to end all love affairs—will change, our babies will become restless teenagers and the ones we love will go away or sicken and die and leave us. If we don't understand and *accept* that everything is changing from moment to moment, that nothing will—or can—remain the same for one click of our fingers, we will try to cling to something that ultimately has no *inherent* existence and we will experience suffering. And throwing tantrums, getting drunk or stoned, hitting someone or something, screaming and smashing things, or even killing won't make the slightest difference, except to produce more suffering for ourselves and others. Even in the face of unavoidable, inevitable death, we cling to being and add mental suffering to our physical last suffering—still greedy for existence as we think we understand it to be.

What of Hatred?
This word, in the context of Buddhist teachings, is better translated as 'aversion'—not wishing to have any association whatever with what is not pleasing. At one end of the scale, aversion can be mere distaste and, at the other end of the scale, it can be murderous intent. Much of what we hate is foreign to our way of seeing things. We fear what we do not understand and what we fear we either run from or seek to destroy. Personally, I find aversion, even a fairly mild type, a difficult condition to handle in some instances. I find there are times when I

have to remind myself that I *know* nothing—that the situation is not necessarily as I, with my flawed senses perceive it. I then try to be tolerant without being condescending. I try to perceive the potential for ultimate enlightenment in every sentient being and to view us all, even the most fortunate, the most self-satisfied as, like myself, subject to dukha.

So-called 'holy' wars (surely a contradiction in terms) are caused by strong aversion to something *other*. This is often something not understood, which arouses a subconscious fear—fear of God's wrath because of the existence of unbelievers, or subconscious fears that other views on religion may threaten the truth of our own beliefs, which we want to see as the only *real* truths.

Anger is part of hatred—a slightly milder form perhaps, but having the potential to develop quickly into full-blown hatred. Anger is a cause of suffering to ourselves first of all; no-one can be joyful or kind while at the same time being angry, and anger eats into us—mentally and physically—like acid. Anger needs to be considered very carefully because of its potential for terrible damage to ourselves and others, and because of the long-lasting consequences of its effects. Many therapies advocate giving expression to one's anger in a controlled situation, with care being taken because of the possibility of hurting oneself or others when the energy of the anger is misdirected through lack of understanding of the causes.

Buddhism has a different way of approaching the problem of angry feelings and this is to analyse the *feeling itself* while it is happening: the actual physical feeling—the way we seem to swell with anger, like a cat raising every hair on end; the feeling of our face burning, heart racing, a feeling in the throat of literally choking with rage. We tremble with the force of our emotion. The Buddhist idea is to make ourselves fully aware of what is going on *within ourselves*. Then we can slow down, as we will when we investigate our feelings; and then the next step becomes possible. We ask, 'What is the *real* cause of my anger?' Quite often it turns out to be nothing more than a bruised ego. Or it can be caused by a deep-seated fear. Next, we need to very, very *honestly* consider our own part in the situation.

This part is not to apportion blame (no judgment is being made) we are merely seeking clarity. Although there is no such thing as simple cause and effect (all conditioned phenomena being of dependent origin) simplifying the picture helps us to see a little more clearly that we are, in part, responsible for this distressing emotion. No-one can *make* me angry—I *choose* to respond to a certain event by becoming angry. I am, or should be, in charge of my own emotions and cannot, in all fairness, blame another person because of *my* emotional responses. Statements such as: '*You* made me angry', '*You* make me so happy', '*You* ruined my life', and so on and so on, are made from a lack of proper understanding of the situation, and because it requires less effort and feels more satisfying to throw the blame, or attribute the cause, to someone or something other than ourselves.

Accepting responsibility for our own contribution to given situations increases our self-respect, our control over our own lives and gives the awareness that we are not powerless—ever. To ignore these benefits is a great pity, yet we all do so. It isn't easy. It takes dedication and continual practice. It can take years, as it did in one of my personal experiences. There was, at one time, a particular person in my life, the very sight of whom came to trigger a hot anger in me. I would feel a burning rage rising from my abdomen at the first angry words from this person. Fortunately for me, I very soon entered a year-long retreat and knew I must deal with this matter first. If I could overcome *this* aversion, others would be child's play.

It eventually worked—one day I was able to stand and listen to the usual verbal abuse in a calm, non-attached manner and, while acknowledging my own part in it, feel compassion replacing all my past anger. Although I did not speak a word in response to the abuse, it was to be the last time it occurred. So I know it works as I speak from personal experience. It is not a matter of wishy-washy, sentimental, martyred forgiveness of the abuser, it is a matter of fully understanding the situation in as wide a sense as possible—all things, or most of them, considered. We come to see that the abuser, like ourselves, is a suffering sentient being. We forgive ourselves for being so ignorant as not to have seen it sooner. Forgiveness is letting go of resentment and the laying of blame. It does not even require personal contact, because the others involved may not have changed and to remain in any relationship with them could be detrimental. We don't ignore the situation; we try to understand it.

Ignorance

So much suffering stems from ignorance. In Buddhist parlance, ignorance does not equate with lack of intelligence or lack of education. It simply implies a not-knowing, a type of confusion, of not being aware of the way phenomena actually exist and therefore why things are the way they have become. It also implies ignorance of the difference between skilful and unskilful behaviour. We are ignorant of the fact that nothing exists inherently of itself.

That is not to say that nothing exists, that it is all mind-games, that I can sit on a railway line safely because trains don't really exist. It is only to say that no *thing* exists. Phenomena or 'things' are dependently arisen—causes are effected by other causes and effects ad infinitum and, into the bargain, don't exist in any particular state for a nano-second. We ignorantly accept *labels* as permanent 'things', for example, 'car', 'house', person named Joan or Andrew, the status quo, or my idea of 'me'. If phenomena can be said to exist at all, it is a momentary existence, almost too momentary to be called existence. The labels—'car', 'house', Joan or whatever I call 'me' and so on—simply indicate a multitudinous group of ever-changing phenomena. Last year's car is not today's car; Joan is not the girl I once knew; I am no longer what I was in the past; and the changes are much quicker than that.

All very interesting indeed, you may say, but what can this offer in the way of helping us cope with *daily* dukha? Well, when all the esotericism and cultural overtones in Buddhism are put aside, the basis of Buddha's compassion remains his wish for us *to free ourselves* from that dukha. But how can this come about? Isn't enlightenment only for saints and hermits? Do we need to emulate the Buddha by leaving home and becoming wandering mendicants? Does becoming non-attached mean giving up our capacity to care for ourselves and others? Is this inner wisdom so much spoken of to be found only in exotic rites and rituals, and endless repeating of texts and prayers in remote foreign monasteries and on top of windswept, snow-covered mountains? Perhaps altitude *does* aid meditation but can't it still be successful at sea-level? If it will take many lifetimes, as asserted by some, to gain enlightenment, why bother? Why not put it off until a later life? Let time take care of it.

Buddha never said we must *all* become monks and nuns before we could become enlightened beings, free from suffering. When he talked to non-monastics he taught them how to escape suffering in their own lives—political, domestic or professional. There *are* advantages for some in seeking a period of isolation in order to study and to assimilate what has been taught, and to teach oneself deep meditation without distraction, but *then* one must do something with what one has learned—put it to skilful use in service to fellow sentient beings, in whatever way suits us best.

There isn't one of us without the potential to develop inner or innate wisdom if only we have the will to do so. One saying has it that we are all Buddhas (enlightened ones) but we just haven't realised it yet, haven't made it real. It is easier to realise this potential when we have happy minds and to have happier minds we need to fully understand our present condition and what we need to do to improve it.

It seems to me—and the view is governed by my own experience—that if we could fully understand the first two Noble Truths and incorporate that understanding in our daily lives, we could be free of dukha. This would require us to become thoroughly aware of whatever action—be it verbal, physical or mental—we are about to undertake *and* the motive or intention behind it. Where the mind goes, actions follow. So first of all we need to understand that *all* sentient beings experience dukha. That is a fact of life and the reason for it is that we were born in the first place. Then we need to see that we suffer because of our uncontrolled desirousness, which has not been directed toward what will bring us and others contentment: happiness and peace of mind.

Also, we very much need to understand anicca (impermanence). What we take for realities are not quite as they seem to be because we are not consciously aware of the state of flux in all conditioned phenomena. We expect what we cling to to remain eternally unchanged and suffer when it is revealed as illusion—illusion concerning what was, in the very first place, an illusion.

If we understood all this, how much more happiness we would experience in life. We would cherish loved ones more, our friends, our fellow beings, our planet home, knowing that they and we are forever changing, that we can never call back the passed moment. All we have is the ever new *now*. Nothing lasts in its apparent form. We can take heart in the fact that even pain and grief do not last in the initial, excruciating form. Memory softens grief in time. All we really have is that which we cannot hold on to, cling to, the *now* moment that has already passed. By letting go of the past moment we can fully use and enjoy the present one, but only if we don't try to hold onto it in turn.

In this talk I have left out much that time does not permit. There is so much that makes sense only to those ready to hear it. There is nothing mysterious about that. It is simply that a person not particularly interested in a given subject does not really hear much of what is said on that subject. It is just the same with the subject of what the Buddha taught. It took me years to understand—in so far as I do—the teaching on emptiness (often referred

to in hushed tones as 'the Void'), and it took just as long
to understand why at that point I had not sprouted a halo
of light and a beatific smile *and* why I could still experience annoyance and sadness. The Dharma is not simply
to be accepted as a terrific philosophical theory—it needs
to be personally experienced to be properly understood.

Don't let my rather cut-and-dried way of discussing it
take all the colour and wonder out of it for anyone. This
is just my way of approach—my personal way.

So, what are we to do? We can begin by:

- Enjoying what we have now but accepting that it is
  already changing.
- Doing no harm to sentient beings—including
  ourselves.
- Learning to control our *own* minds rather than our
  neighbour's mind.
- Seeing that the world is in part our personal mind construct. (We see existence according to our personal
  mental outlook; it seems to be miserable under good
  conditions for some, and good under miserable conditions for others.)

We are all different psychologically but we are all seeking
happiness. We would all like to experience paradise
now—and the tantalising truth is that we could have it if
only we knew where to begin looking for it. Here is a
little poem which I think says a lot about that:

Seeking Paradise we find Paradise a state of mind.
What is bliss sublime for me, endless boredom is for thee.
But deep within us Wisdom lies, wider, clearer than the
    skies.

Seek, not from another's tongue—Seek 'til deep within is
   rung.
The wisdom bell—that has no sound—and Paradise is
   all around.

In finishing, let me request you to disbelieve everything
I have said until you have investigated it for yourselves.
Thank you for listening—and may you all be blessed.

October 1996

Namo Buddhaya

WHAT DID BUDDHA SAKYAMUNI TEACH?

Thank you for being here. Let us all close our eyes for a few moments while we leave our daily concerns aside. Make no effort but simply do not follow the thoughts that arise.

As Dorthy Darby has just told you, I am a fully ordained bhikkhuni, a Buddhist nun. I was first ordained into the Tibetan tradition by Tenzin Gyatso, His Holiness the fourteenth Dalai Lama and six high lamas, and later into the Vietnamese tradition by the Patriarch of Vietnam, Master Thich Huyen Vi and ten male and female elders. The second ordination was necessary as I wished to receive highest ordination. The Theravadin and Tibetan traditions do not hold this lineage for women. As to what tradition I may now be said to belong, I prefer to be known as what I call a Buddha Buddhist.

I am one of a very loose group known as wandering monks and nuns who do not often live in organised monasteries and who teach whenever requested to do so. When one gives up the support of the monastic life, one does the best one can according to one's means. I do voluntary work in the community. I do not shave my head these days, having found my hair seems to give me better rapport with my Western fellow citizens and clients.

It is a pleasure to speak about the Dharma to people like yourselves—open-minded, willing to listen to different ideas, people who think. Thinking is a very rare activity.

Thinking is what the Buddha tried to teach—thinking about existence, not in the manner of perpetually worrying and speculating, but of being *fully* aware of the way things have become in any given moment.

When something happens to us, an event, something with which we are personally concerned, it is wise to consider how the present situation arose, instead of reacting blindly out of greed, hatred, ignorance or fear. In other words, to *think* about it, to be as aware as possible of the causes and implications, and to make sure our reactions are appropriate and useful.

Buddha did not want people to have faith in what he said simply because he was awakened, or to believe what he told them without their thinking about it for themselves.

Who was the Buddha? What made him wish to teach and just what was it he taught? Before I get to that, I am sorry to have to tell those of you who cherish an image, in porcelain or brass, of a fat, laughing Oriental, that this is not a representative of Sakyamuni Buddha but of the Chinese god of wealth and happiness, things which are indicated by obesity or the possession of abundance, and by mirth showing enjoyment of a happy life.

There are many stories of the early life of the Buddha, mostly legend and folklore, with universal type religious overtones: the pure birth from Queen Maya's side; the words spoken by the newly born infant and the steps taken toward the compass points; the story of Siddartha never becoming aware of sickness, poverty and death until adulthood; his prophetic horoscope; and his leaving behind him a newly born son and sneaking off into the night, never to return to his home as a son, husband or father.

From widespread reading and study of the political/religious/social conditions in India in the sixth century BC, plus the interpretation of some archaeological finds, it is more likely that the son of Rajah Suddodhana and Rani Maya (his first wife) was possibly born by caesarean section and needed assistance to breathe. It is written in the oldest texts that the infant was washed in cold and warm water—in that order. The water came from the tank in the Lumbini Gardens where Maya, on her way back to her family home for the birth, as was the custom, went into labour. Those tanks, as many of you will have seen, are stone-lined pools and hardly sterile. I am a midwife, or was, and a trained nurse, and I see the babe being splashed with cold water from the tank to stimulate respiration (still a common practice) rather than being bathed in warm water as any newborn infant is bathed.

Meanwhile, the Rani was washed with the tank water and developed puerperal or post-operative sepsis and died after seven days. The child was reared and possibly suckled by Maya's sister (Suddodhana's second wife), already the mother of a son, Davida, the wicked, jealous half-brother of Siddhartha. Davida later tried unsuccessfully to kill his rival sibling and gathered a following of his own, attempting to discredit Siddhartha and his teachings.

As for the Buddha leaving a newborn son, it behoves us to consider the customs of his day which survive still: early marriage and an heir as soon as possible by the first wife, irrespective of any children born to concubines, or daughters born even to the principal wife. Many hand-maidens were part of Yasodarah's dowry, but we have no record of other children as other sons would not be the heir (as in Davida's case) and daughters were seldom listed unless something spectacular happened to them. Is this mere speculation? Possibly. But, we do have a funerary urn, found at Piprawah last century, with this inscription:

> This is the urn of the relics of the Bhagavat, the
> Buddha of the Sakya tribe, that is enshrined (by
> honourable brothers and sisters, wives and children).

Note the sequence of the wording.

Be that as it may, Siddhartha Gautama did what was the norm for his place and caste and time: he trained as a warrior and future leader of his tribe; he was well educated by the best available tutors in religion, politics and economics; he married suitably and produced a legal heir, Rahula. Having done this, he was free to become a so-called 'homeless one', a wandering seeker-after-wisdom. He was by then no discontented youth; he was a deep thinker and twenty-nine years of age. He left his home, as again was often the custom, and spent the next seven years learning from the wisest and most well-known religious and philosophical teachers of India, trying out for himself all their methods of gaining insight into the fundamental principles of existence and the cause of human suffering.

There was nothing unusual about his behaviour considering his times and his position in society. Only the wealthy and well-off could provide for their dependants adequately during their absence or have the educational preparation in philosophical thought to be drawn to the quest for greater wisdom.

Finding that what he learned from his teachers failed in the end to satisfy his intellectual thirst, he determined to break through or perish in the attempt. Finally, he relinquished intellectual process and argument and, by then mentally exhausted, he quietened his mind and—just as we often find the answer to a worrisome problem when we give up battling with it—Siddhartha made that breakthrough. Now he was the Buddha, the awakened one.

So, here we have a normal human being born of human parents, who fulfilled all the functions of man—nothing supernatural, unless one considers his great courage, determination, intellectual capacity and universal compassion as being above the merely 'normal'.

What was it, in terms that make sense for us today, that this man considered worth trying to teach to those who wished to listen? Leaving aside the almost submerging accretions of later philosophical arguments and different cultural overtones, here are the main, and as far as we have been able to discover, the earliest teachings of the Buddha. There are no divine commandments, no threat of eternal damnation and, likewise, no promises of a perfect happy ending. There *is* moral and ethical advice, and explanations of karma—action and reaction.

The rules for monastic living are necessary for the smooth running of any organisation. They are not necessarily useful for the attainment of enlightenment. That attainment will be a deeply personal experience and cannot be formulated by rules and regulations like a well-run railway system—leave Station A at such and such a time, and arrive at Station Z at such and such a time, with only designated stops along the way. Monastic rules have their use only in helping to develop self-discipline and powers of concentration.

There is no time limit, either way, for the attainment

of enlightenment from the time of one's first intention. It may take a lifetime, yet, if one is ready, it may come as an almost instantaneous, blinding flash of insight.

The teachings given to Buddha's very first listeners seem to have been on impermanence and the emptiness of inherent existence of all compound phenomena, but these listeners were already advanced philosophers and yogis. For us, it is easier to begin with the Four Noble Truths (or Truths of the Noble Ones, which is a better translation) and the Eightfold Path of conduct. Let me repeat the Four Noble Truths. They are:

1. This truth is dukha. Existence is lacking in lasting satisfaction. Dukha is not getting what we want and having to suffer what we don't want. Dukha is old age, sickness and death, lamentation and the ungraspableness of phenomena. No matter how fortunate in worldly goods, health, fame and talent beings may be, they can never escape dukha. *This* existence of ours *is* dukha. Or one could say that dukha *is* existence.

2. This truth states that there is a cause of dukha and that cause is craving, wanting—desirousness. This desirousness is needed initially for our survival. Without it we would perish. But, once we have become independent beings, this craving is no longer necessary to the same degree and becomes the cause of suffering or dukha. We are never satisfied. No amount of wealth, beauty or love is ever enough. We ignore what we *do* have in our craving for what we *do not* have, often craving what is quite impossible for us to *ever* have.

Oh, doom! Oh, gloom! Isn't Buddhism a woeful philosophy, just as you always knew it was? But wait! There is more!

3. This truth tells us there is a way out of all this craving and consequent suffering, a way to live happier lives and to be more successful in what we undertake to achieve.
4. This truth suggests that if we follow the Eightfold Path, we will begin to see the way out of dukha.

The Eightfold Path was taught in several different ways, depending on the philosophical level of the hearer, but the basic steps remain the same. They are:

1. Right views, free of superstition.
2. Right thought, high and worthy of the intelligent and worthy person.
3. Right speech, open, truthful. (Is it kind? Is it true? Is it necessary? Confession may be good for *our* souls but it may not be so for the hearer.)
4. Right action in all concerns of life.
5. Right livelihood, bringing no danger to living beings. (Buddhists refrain from working with poisons, in the armaments industry and in butchery.)
6. Right effort in all the other seven steps.
7. Right mindfulness, the watchful, attentive mind not easily distracted by novelty and show.
8. Right contemplation of the deep matters of life.

There is, surely, nothing mysterious or difficult about these teachings, and just think what harmony they would bring to worldly existence if we could follow them to the best of our individual ability without becoming dogmatic over semantics and philosophical speculation. There is, surely, nothing harmful in this, nothing threatening to whatever religious beliefs others might hold. All that is asked of the hearer is that they test the Dharma personally and accept nothing until it makes sense to their own mind.

Next, Buddha Sakyamuni taught, to those with the capacity to understand them, impermanence and the emptiness of inherent existence of all compound phenomena, often spoken of as dependent origination, that no 'thing' exists. I will speak of these teachings in order, although they are thoroughly entwined with each other as well as with the Four Noble Truths.

Impermanence. It is a fact, to which we pay little heed in our everyday lives, that nothing—nothing at all—remains the same for even less than a nanosecond. Nothing. Not a seed; not a blade of grass; not a tongue of flame; not the most beautiful object; not the strongest passion; not the sharpest sorrow; not our bodies; not our ideas, nor even our opinions. Whether we are aware of it or not, everything is in a constant state of change, even down to gold bars and steel girders. Much, even most, of our pain and suffering can be attributed to our ignorance of or denial of impermanence. When we are in trouble we often despair, feeling that there is no way out, that the misery will go on forever, that the pain, perhaps of bereavement, will never soften. Sometimes we feel that even death will not release us from our suffering. Yet the situation, whatever it may be, is constantly changing, sometimes for the better, although our depression often leaves us blind to such a possibility.

The other side of this picture is the expectation that what we *grasp* at is unchangeable. We do not see that our most prized possessions are dissolving before our eyes. When we begin to become even faintly aware that this is so, we seek to lay the blame on anything but the

law of impermanence. When warm friendships cool or
lose intensity, we suffer, as we do when love affairs and
relationships change. We may be experiencing an expansion of business matters and expect that expansion to
continue without altering—except to our own advantage.
If we were able to accept fully the fact of impermanence,
we would realise (even respecting the things we would
like to avoid and that seem to be trapping us) that things
are changing all the time and if we are aware and act
skilfully, things may turn out better than at first seemed
possible.

With respect to those things we want to remain completely unchanged, we would realise that this is impossible. We would come to see that all we really have is
now: the given moment. How much more we would
appreciate what *is* now. How dear to us would be our
families, our loves, our friends, our fellow beings, and
our own planet home. How wisely we would spend our
smiles, kind words and acts. The *realisation* (the making
real to our minds) of the law of impermanence could
enlighten us all and lessen the pains of unavoidable
dukha for ourselves and for others. How childish, futile
and unnecessary our personal aversions and squabbles
would seem, and how wasted the energy we put into
carrying burdens of unresolved guilt and resentment from
the past.

On now to dependent origination or the emptiness of
inherent existence of all compound phenomena.

When I first became interested in Buddhism, some
forty years ago, I could not grasp this teaching at all and
decided that, rather than carry on trying to imagine what
I had heard spoken of in awed tones as 'the Void' (some
metaphysical *non*-phenomena) I would put the question

aside and come back to it later. I never consciously did so, but as my Buddhist education advanced I must have learned something. One day it quite suddenly occurred to me that I had imagined this teaching to be mysterious knowledge far beyond my capability to grasp. I now see that, because of this attitude, I hadn't really listened or applied my mind to what I heard, because it quite suddenly came clear and I heard myself giving the correct answer to a question put to me on the subject. I said the words 'Emptiness of *inherent* existence—nothing existing from its own side—dependent origination'. Everything, every event, all phenomena coming into and going out of existence depends on everything else, which, in turn, does likewise. A marvellous web of being.

But of what use is such esoteric knowledge in the everyday life of sentient beings—of you and me with all our problems? In the first place, it shows us what karma, as spoken of by the Buddha, really is: not some supernatural form of punishment and reward accruing to us in future lifetimes, but the fact of our actions of body, speech and mind being dependent on all phenomena for their coming into existence and, in turn, having their effect on everything else. We see this in everyday life, when one person in a family or team, or a group of friends, is in a particularly pleasant or nasty mood. The mood occurs from many causes and in turn has many effects. These effects ripple outward with sometimes infinitesimal vibrations. This is happening all the time, everywhere, and is the reason the world is as it is or has become at any moment. Each of us contributes skilfully or unskilfully. Each of us is, in part, responsible. The effects of our actions are often immediately apparent but, on the other hand, we ourselves may never become consciously aware of them. We may be, and so often are, giving help or causing trouble without realising it.

These are the basic and most important parts of the Buddha's teachings for, without fully understanding these teachings we cannot proceed to the deeper teachings. Many people make the mistake of chasing around the world after teachers who will initiate them into the esoteric mysteries of Buddhist religion, mistaking this for a quick road to enlightenment. I know that road only too well. It comes before one fully realises, truly understands, that the path begins right here and now from within ourselves. We try to build the top storey of the building before we have made solid foundations. Of course, digging out the ground and setting solid foundations is hard work and means transforming our own minds. It seems much easier to get someone else to say some mysterious words over us. At initiations, we take the symbols and mantras to be magic formulas that will save us many steps. No-one can *give* us enlightenment. Concentration and meditation are the way to go. It is not a matter of having faith in, or believing the Buddha's teachings. It is a matter of fully understanding them.

When this existence—samsara or the unenlightened condition—is said to be mere illusion, this means simply that existence is not as we are accustomed to view it. We view the world without awareness of dependent origination and impermanence, and so accept illusion for reality. We live our lives accordingly, clinging to illusions like trying to grasp the lover in a dream. We see things the way we think they *are*, or *should* be, and act in error. We are like bulls in china shops in our dealings with existence. We think that lightning-quick reactions are always wise. They are only wise (or skilful) when we are fully aware of the circumstances surrounding an event. The daily news is an example of this, where we rush in to feed and arm a group so it may defend itself against the 'enemy' and, before long, find our 'victims' are the new aggressors. The lesson here is not that we should close our minds to suffering but that we should take care before rushing in and creating something worse than what we tried to cure.

In our human ignorance we are so sure we know everything, yet we don't even know the thoughts and true feelings of the person sitting next to us, nor do we really understand our own.

With my pragmatic way of speaking of the Dharma it may seem I am denying any spiritual value to be found in Buddhism. This would be wrong for me to do. There is colour and wonder and a deep mysticism in the Dharma. Mysticism is usually thought of as exclusive to theistic religions. That is not so. True mystics are actually beyond religion. They have travelled further than the average seeker but what they learn can only be translated into the language of religion if it is not to remain unintelligible. If this isn't done, the mystic becomes the star turn at the next public bonfire celebration, considered a witch or wizard. How could that which cannot even be thought be explained? Through music, perhaps, or allegorical paintings, sculpture, and sometimes through poetry and prose, but obliquely. There are many ways, yet they are still only signposts. The moon's reflection in still water is lovely and inspiring but the reflection is not the moon nor is the treasure map the treasure. All the words, pictures, chanting, statues, mandalas, bells, drums, gongs, candles and lamps and incense can only assist our one-pointed concentration and be signposts.

Most of us find it easier to sit, even in full-lotus position, our hands upturned in our laps, looking pious, and
just lean on the signpost. This is our individual choice,
of course: to remain at ease or to dare to journey onward.
The first step, if we decide to take it, is to understand
ourselves and our motives for what we do. Until we have
analysed the reasons for our own thoughts, words and
deeds, with scrupulous honesty, we cannot be said to
really understand anything else. Once this—the most
difficult and painful step—has been taken, all the rest
becomes easier. It is as though we had cleared a thorny
bramble from our path.

Once we have cleared the garbage from our minds,
dropped our heavy backpacks of guilts and old resent-
ments, and stopped trying to be omniscient, all one can
say is that it is amazing what can now enter the mind
unhindered and, seemingly, unsought. What enters is not
from 'outside', from 'other' powers; it is the freeing of our
own intuition, our own inner wisdom that has always
been there.

Buddhism preaches no dogmatic, absolute truths to
be imposed on anyone, so there is no quarrel between
Buddhist and non-Buddhist. What you believe is not my
business. For this reason, the Dharma is taught only on
request.

Buddhists can be infuriating in that they will never
really tell you anything until you ask. This is simply
because the way the question is formulated allows the
teacher to gain an idea of where you are 'at', as it
were. Then the answer can be given as clearly as possible for that particular questioner. It was for this reason
that the Buddha often gave the same teaching in a
slightly different way. One does not speak to an

engineer in the language of the neurologist, for example.

The ethics enshrined in the Eightfold Path and the precepts taken by Buddhists can form the basis of a decent, worthwhile life for anyone, no matter what their religion, and can return a fair amount of human contentment, and even some of what we call 'happiness'. All this, even in the midst of inevitable, inescapable dukha.

Before I close, I would like to make a request of you. Please, do not believe a word I have spoken here, but investigate for yourselves.

Thank you for listening. May you be blessed.

April 1997

A FINAL WORD

It is the writer's fervent wish that the foregoing short discourse on Buddhism, both religious and philosophical, might lift, for those interested, some of the obscuring veils of cultural additions to the original teachings.

I hope, also, that it will go some way toward helping develop tolerance for a religion that is no threat to any other, whether in this country or elsewhere. Diverse cultures, diverse religions and diverse races make for a wonderfully colourful world. Long may it be so.

I would not be a true Buddhist if I did not hope that amongst my readers there will be some who wish to know more. It is no longer necessary to seek in hidden, far-off places, to climb steep mountains in search of wisdom. All that is needed is the sincere desire to learn, then the way will be opened.

Knowledge casts out the fear and intolerance that the unknown or the not-understood engenders. Intolerance on one side strengthens intolerance on the other.

I have added a very short list of suggested reading—something to get started on. Who knows where it will lead you? There is so much we do not—cannot—know in our present ignorant state of being.

A request before I lay down my pen. Do not believe a word I have said. I am no scholar, no guru. Investigate for yourself and keep on doing so.

SUGGESTED READING LIST

As this book is not written in order to teach anyone Buddhist philosophy, merely to whet the appetite of those so interested, there is no particular work recommended as a beginning. It really does not matter where one begins because, if the interest is there, one choice will lead to others.

A History of Buddhist Philosophy, David J. Kalapahana, University of Hawaii Press, Honolulu, Hawaii, 1992

Born in Tibet, Chogyam Trungpa, Allen & Unwin Paperbacks, London, 1997

Buddhist Studies Review, copies obtainable from R. Webb, 31 Russell Chambers, Bury Place, London WC1A 2JK

Freedom in Exile, autobiography of H.H. The Dalai Lama, Hodder & Stoughton, London, 1990

Good, Evil and Beyond, P.A. Payutto, tr. Bruce Evans, Buddhadhamma Foundation, Bangkok, 1996

Philosophy of the Buddha, Professor A.J. Bahm, Rider & Co, 1958

Studies in the Origins of Buddhism, 2nd edition, G.C. Pande, Molilal Banarsides, Delhi, 1974

The Beginnings of Buddhism, Kogen Mizuno, tr. Richard L. Gage, Kosei Publishing Co. Tokyo, 1992

The Book of Kindred Sayings, tr. F.L. Woodward, Pali Text Society, London, 1975

The Buddha, Trevor Ling, Temple Smith, London, 1973

The Diamond Sutra and the Sutra of Hui Neng, tr. A.F. Price and Wong Mou-Lam, Shambala, Colorado, USA, 1977

The Dawn of Tantra, Herbert V. Guenther & Chogyam Trungpa, Berkeley, California, 1975

The Faith to Doubt, Stephen Batchelor, Parrallax Press, Berkeley, California, 1990

The Good Heart, H.H. The Dalai Lama & Don L. Freeman, Wisdom Publications, London, 1998

The Life and Works of Sariputta Thera, 2nd edition, tr. Dr Thich Huyen-Vi, Linh-Son Research Institute, France, 1989

The Long Discourses of the Buddha, tr. Maurice Walsh, Wilsdom Publications, London, 1987

The Nature of Buddhist Ethics, Damien Keown, Macmillan Press, London, 1992

The Tibetan Book of Living and Dying, Sogyal Rinpoche, Rider (Random House), London, 1995

The Tibetan Book of the Dead, tr. W.Y. Evans-Wentz, Oxford University Press, Oxford, 1982

What the Buddha Taught, Walpola Rahula, Grove Press, New York, 1983

7